BARRIERS TO INTIMACY

BARRIERS TO INTIMACY

for People Torn by Addiction

GAYLE ROSELLINI AND **MARK WORDEN**

■ HAZELDEN®

First Published June 1989

ISBN: 0-89486-592-7
Library of Congress Catalog Card Number: 88-84117

Printed in the United States of America

Editor's Note:
Hazelden Educational Materials offers a variety of information on chemical dependency and related areas. Our
publications do not necessarily represent Hazelden or its
programs, nor do they officially speak for any Twelve Step
organization.

To Horsetoof & Jowls
without whose good bad examples
this book could not have been written

Contents

Acknowledgments

This book could not have been written without the assistance of Alta Crawford, Gail Pickle, DeeAnn Melevin, Lenore and William Horden, Patrice Morrison, Alan Martin, and the late Bill Morrison. Susinski and our good friend and neighbor, Doris Steinhauer, deserve special mention. We would also like to thank our editors at Hazelden. Brian Lynch encouraged us to continue when we despaired. Sid Farrar stood up for us. And Jeff Petersen and Don Freeman undangled our participles and uncomplicated our complications without beating us over the head with *The Chicago Manual of Style.* Thank you, guys.

The stories you are about to read are true. The names have been changed to protect the guilty.

We gratefully acknowledge the following for permission to quote from the materials listed:

Gracie: A Love Story, by George Burns. Used by permission of Putnam Publishing Group. ©1988 by George Burns.

Marital Myths: Two Dozen Mistaken Beliefs That Can Ruin A Marriage (Or Make A Bad One Worse). ©1985 by Arnold A. Lazarus. Reproduced for Hazelden Educational Materials by permission of Impact Publishers, Inc., P.O. Box 1094, San Luis Obispo, CA 93401. Further reproduction prohibited.

Alcoholics Anonymous, New York: Alcoholics Anonymous World Services, Inc., Second Edition, 1955.

Alcoholics Anonymous Comes of Age, New York: Alcoholics Anonymous World Services, Inc., 1957.

Feelings: Our Vital Signs, Willard Gaylin, New York: Harper & Row Publishers (Ballantine Books Edition), 1979. ©1979 by Willard Gaylin, M.D.

Introduction

Intimacy is a hot topic.

While women tend to be more willing to discuss relationships, men are also interested in the subject of intimacy. Not long ago, a friend expressed his dismay about the concept of intimacy: "It just seems so jumbled together," he complained. "Who makes up the rules about intimacy? Who sets the standards about 'appropriate' and 'inappropriate' intimate behavior? How do we know when we have the 'right' amount of intimacy with a partner? Is it possible that some people would never be satisfied?"

These are all good questions, and there are no simple answers. Different cultures have widely varying standards of intimacy between the sexes. Men and women differ in their ideas and ideals about intimacy, which often leads to misunderstanding and conflict. And there are vast differences between individuals in their need for various forms of intimacy.

Love After Addiction

Chemical dependency has a destructive effect on all aspects of a person's life. *Barriers to Intimacy* is our attempt to give a positive answer to the question: "Is there love after addiction?"

In writing this book, we talked with men and women recovering from addictions — single people, married people, divorced people, and the widowed. We listened while codependents, often in tears, related their sagas of turmoil and confusion. And we benefited from the observations and insights of friends and relatives. (Throughout this book we have changed the names and other identifying information to ensure the anonymity of those who told us their stories.)

When we told people we were writing a book about intimacy, they were usually eager to share their own experiences. A typical pattern developed: At first the conversation would be full of socially acceptable comments. "Yes, since Robert and I went into chemical dependency treatment our life together has gotten happier and happier." As the conversation progressed, the person would become visibly upset. Soon there would be an avalanche of emotion — tears, anger, despair. When these recovering people started really talking about their intimate lives what they usually expressed was *anger* and *pain*.

Many of our conversations took place in a quiet restaurant over lunch. The waitresses got used to seeing Gayle meeting a number of different people for lunches that lasted as long as four hours. After about a month of this, an embarrassed waitress approached Gayle as she entered the restaurant. "Here," she said, handing Gayle a box of Kleenex. "Will you please ask your friends to use these instead of our linen napkins as handkerchiefs? We're having a hard time getting the mascara out of the cloth."

Gayle says, "I think the only reason I wasn't asked to take my business someplace else is because I always left a large tip."

Habit: The Ultimate Barrier to Intimacy

It's one thing to acknowledge that real problems of intimacy exist, and quite another to make the changes that improve the quality of an intimate relationship. The major reason is *habit*. When you look at relationships closely and analyze the behavior that makes up intimacy, you'll find that habits lie at the core of intimate problems — habits of thought, habits of action. The major barriers to intimacy stem from habits that are deeply rooted in fear, anger, and issues of power and control.

We are interested in exploring the barriers to intimacy that occur as a direct consequence of chemical dependency or as the result of living with someone who has been enmeshed in chemical dependency.

More specifically, this is a self-help guide for individuals whose lives have been conflicted by chemical dependency. This includes:

- Recovering people . . .
- People who have been in love or married to a chemically dependent person . . .
- People who grew up with a chemically dependent person in the family . . .

We take *intimacy in recovery* as our starting point, for we believe that intimacy is difficult, if not impossible, to achieve and maintain in relationships where chemical dependency continues. The very nature of chemical dependency breeds distrust, secrecy, dishonesty, suspicion, and fear. Thus, our rule: *Drug-free first, then intimacy.*

This is a crucial point in any discussion of intimacy, because drug-affected behavior cripples and often kills intimacy in relationships.

If you or your partner are caught in the downward spiral of alcoholism or other drug abuse, concentrate on recovery first. Then, in time, there will be a fertile ground for intimacy to take root and grow.

It's important to keep in mind that recovery makes intimacy possible, but recovery does not guarantee intimacy. People who have grown apart under the stress of chemical dependency do not automatically become intimate as recovery progresses.

In the course of chemical dependency, we become strangers to friends, family, and other loved ones. And that strangeness often persists far into recovery. Old habits die hard.

There are many kinds of intimacy, many varieties of intimate behavior. Our goal is not to urge folks to settle for only the most perfect form of intimacy, but to encourage people to see the many small ways of diminishing the barriers that keep them feeling alone and unloved.

We have written this book as a self-help guide for individuals. Although intimacy involves at least two people, we believe the only person we have the power to change reliably is ourselves. So throughout this book, we encourage readers to examine their lives for behaviors, beliefs, and attitudes that create barriers to intimacy.

We offer positive alternatives to overcome those barriers. And we provide information that can help a confused person understand why people who love each other often destroy intimacy by acting like selfish, insensitive, or demanding jerks.

This, then, is our premise:

> *Chemical dependency, in and of itself, creates anti-intimate behaviors — **barriers to intimacy** — in the chemically dependent person, in family members, and in other loved ones.*

Denial, deceit, distrust, anger, fear, and suspicion are part and parcel of alcoholism, other addictions, and codependency. These negative ways of interacting with loved ones don't necessarily improve just because a person gets sober or straight.

Those who have lived in the shadow of chemical dependency, and who want intimacy with others, must become aware of their own habitual anti-intimate behaviors. More: They must make a concerted effort to change, to behave in ways that foster intimacy.

Of Brutes and Victims

A popular message lately in books and articles about intimacy goes something like this: Men are brutes and women are poor victims — tragic figures who get swept away, who love too much. Our experiences tell us that women can be pretty brutish at times, and men know how to play the victim role to the hilt. But it's sometimes hard to tell who's the brute and who's the victim because we have gender-specific ways of expressing these two characteristics. Instead of looking at cultural stereotypes and fantasies, we want to look at the specific behavior of real people in real situations.

The fundamental message of this book is one of individual responsibility. We believe that abandoning the victim stance and eliminating the power games of manipulation and intimidation are absolutely essential to personal growth — for both men and women.

In almost all intimate relationships conflicted by chemical dependency there is a push-pull mentality. A combination of desire and fear. A yearning for oneness and a longing for freedom. A need to control combined with unhealthy dependence.

All these feelings are normal, but they can frighten us if we don't understand them. And they can destroy intimacy if we fail to understand the importance of *compromise* if we expect to happily live with or love another person.

The most exciting part of writing this book was watching recovering men and women reclaiming their lost capacity to give and receive love unselfishly. As one man said, "It's as though I stepped out of the dark into the sunlight. At first I recoiled. I was used to the dark, used to being alone. But the sun warmed me, allowed me to see and feel things that I had been blind to before. To me, love is just like the sun. And, as we all know, without the sun there is no life."

Yes, there is love after addiction.

Finally, a personal note: This book reflects our personal philosophy about intimacy — a philosophy based on real behavior in day-to-day relationships. Our point of view has evolved as we worked together in the chemical dependency field, and as we lived together as partners, mates, best friends, critics, confidantes, and lovers — a seventeen-year drug-free monogamous relationship, rich in dachshunds, computers, books, herbaceous borders, and quockerwodgers — Gooeyduckese for "ducks." ("Gooeyduck — or Gooeydunck — is a private family lingo. Every family should have one.) A relationship with ups, downs, loop-the-loops, and a few tricky quantum leaps that defied gravity. We hope our ideas on intimacy will be useful for others.

CHAPTER ONE

A Scene From a Marriage

Jack wanted sex. His wife, Audrey, was ignoring him.

Jack was propped up on pillows watching the late news on the small bedroom television and if Audrey didn't come to bed pretty soon he was going to be too sleepy to do anything. She was in the kitchen packing lunches for tomorrow. Jack could tell from the way she was pulling out drawers and slamming the cupboard doors that she was still ticked off at him.

Jack was ticked off too. What was her problem, anyway? Why did women always have to make such a big deal out of nothing? All he'd done was make an innocent little comment about how big her butt was getting — a harmless joke, that's all it was — and Audrey had to turn it into a big discussion about the entire nature of their relationship. No sense of humor, that was Audrey's problem.

Maybe she was getting her period. Yeah, that could be it. Her period always made her bitchy and hysterical. Every twenty-eight days or so she'd get on this kick about what a jerk he was and how he never made time for *their relationship*. Then she'd go on and on about how he didn't really care about her feelings. What a bunch of crap! The thing that ticked him off most was the way she accused him of always trying to put her down instead of listening to what she had to say.

Oh, he listened, all right. He heard every word. It was like she had this unending list of things for him to do: Take out the garbage, mow the lawn, work on their relationship.

Relationship. What did that word mean, anyway? No matter what he did or said, Audrey was always dissatisfied with their relationship. It was enough to make him barf. Why was she always trying to get him to show more emotion? Why did she always need reassurance? He'd married her, hadn't he? He'd stuck with her, hadn't he? What better proof did she need that he loved her?

Sure they'd had some bad years — his drinking years — but that was behind them. As far as he was concerned, things were fine now, so why was she always complaining?

Sometimes Jack wished he could just make Audrey shut up like he used to back in the drinking days. It was easy then. The alcohol, coursing through his blood like high-octane jet fuel, dissolved all his scared-boy anxieties. Nothing mattered except getting what he wanted. He felt like a man then, not afraid of anyone, not afraid to tell Audrey to back off. Unfortunately, that I-don't-care-what-anyone-thinks-about-me attitude had cost him a job and almost destroyed his marriage. And that brought on enough scared-boy anxieties to just about kill him.

But that was in the past. He was working again, and he was sober. Still, there were times when he longed to recapture some of that old drunken brashness — some of the old jaunty self-confidence that got him what he wanted when he wanted it. Audrey was going to have to understand that just because he'd quit drinking, he hadn't turned into a wimp. No way. Underneath the Easy Does It attitude of his sobriety, the old wild man was still lurking around, waiting for a chance to come out and bust some heads.

Audrey came into the bedroom wearing her dark blue flannel nightgown, the one that looked like a nun's habit. It fit like a loose sack and buttoned clear up under her chin. She might as well have come to bed carrying a sign emblazoned with the words *DON'T TOUCH ME.*

Jack watched her closely as she pulled back the covers and climbed into bed.

"Good night," she said, turning her back to him. "Don't watch television for too long, okay? I'm tired."

"You're not still mad at me, are you, babe?"

8

"No," Audrey said, obviously meaning yes.

Jack's hand found her hip under the covers. "Well, then, how about it?"

Audrey turned over suddenly, offering him a thin, hard smile. Jack recoiled, startled by her anger.

"What are you so mad about, honey?" he asked innocently. "I didn't do anything."

"An hour ago you called me a fat pig, and now you expect me to come to bed for fun and games as if nothing happened."

"It was a joke, babe, that's all."

"It wasn't funny."

"Dammit, Audrey!"

"Why are you shouting?"

"Because you seem determined to pick a fight," he said hotly. "So, okay, let's fight. I'm getting sick and tired of you turning every little thing I say into proof that I'm the world's biggest jerk. You don't like our relationship? Well, the front door swings both ways, baby. Don't let it hit you in the butt on your way out."

"Is that what you want?" Her face was bland, but she was dismayed inside. Why did every argument have to come down to this? Why couldn't they ever just talk like a couple of rational human beings?

Jack was silent a long time. He fiddled with the remote control for the television, but he didn't turn it off. Finally he said, "If it's what *you* want."

Audrey sighed. She could roll over now and go to sleep in icy silence or she could take Jack's hand, hold it, place it against her breast, and close the breach between them. She took his hand. Jack smiled and moved closer to her.

Audrey lay on her back and, as Jack's hands traveled over her in the familiar pattern, felt a little bit of her self-respect wither and die. How could she love Jack so much, and hate him at the same time?

She allowed her body to move gently against his, her soft sighs and moans coming automatically at just the proper moments, but her thoughts were a thousand miles away.

Could I make it on my own? Audrey wondered. *Could I support myself and the kids on what I make? Even with child support it would be awfully hard.*

She felt the tip of Jack's tongue on her earlobe, so she gasped loudly enough to please him. The reporter on television said the weather tomorrow would be cold and clear. *It would be a good day to wear her new sweater,* Audrey thought. *Jack would be furious if he knew how much she had really paid for it, but she worked hard and she deserved to do something nice for herself once in a while.*

That thought brought her back to the reality of the moment with something like a thud. She pressed herself against Jack, hoping he'd finish quickly, before the broken mattress spring poked a hole in her back and the smell of his sweat got to her. Next time she'd make him take a shower first. Finally, with a heavy sigh of satisfaction, Jack rolled onto his side.

Later, he smoked a high-tar cigarette and stroked her thigh gently. "Did you?" he whispered.

"Couldn't you tell?" she answered coyly, then nuzzled him to make the lie believable.

He patted her leg twice and rolled over. He was asleep in three minutes.

Audrey got up and turned off the TV on her way to the bathroom. Her bladder felt sore and irritated. Was it a bladder infection again? She hoped she wouldn't have to go back to the doctor for another dose of antibiotics. *And they lived happily ever after.* Audrey laughed bitterly at her small joke as she crawled back into bed.

Intimate Relationships: A Major Problem in Recovery

We've just taken a glimpse inside a real marriage — into the secret lives of Jack and Audrey. They have disclosed thoughts and feelings they kept hidden from each other for years. They realize this scene is not a flattering portrait of them, either as individuals or as a couple. Yet, they are willing to share their experiences with us because through hard work and personal change they have managed to transform an empty and bitter marriage into a love affair.

It wasn't easy. During the first ten years of their marriage, they were deeply enmeshed in chemical dependency and all the pain and loneliness that accompanies it. Jack drank too much and he smoked marijuana. Audrey just about went crazy trying to control his outrageous behavior, trying to hold the family together, and trying to be the perfect wife and mother.

When Jack finally got sober, they both thought their marriage would improve. It did. A little bit. Audrey no longer made herself sick waiting for Jack to come home. She no longer jumped every time the phone rang. Jack didn't wake up every morning coughing and retching. His mind grew sharp and clear.

Things *were* better. As Audrey put it, "With sobriety, our marriage went from worse to bad. It was an improvement, but it wasn't enough. I felt disappointed and cheated almost every day."

Perhaps you, too, have suffered the same sort of disappointment Audrey felt. If you have lived under the shadow of chemical dependency — as an addict or as the child or spouse of an addict — you may have expected involvement in a recovery program to turn your troubled love life into a richly rewarding experience.

But, as you may have discovered by now, intimate relationships can still remain a major problem area for recovering people. Why? Because despite the impressive improvements that come with recovery, we are hardly infallible or perfect beings. We are still plagued by fears and guilt trips and emotional hang-ups. And some of us are still bleeding from the wounds of the past.

In short, we are people in the process of healing and discovery, not faultless and charming characters out of the pages of a romance novel. Many of us have no idea how to conduct ourselves in an intimate relationship without the use of intoxicants to soften the harsh realities of close relationships — bad breath, rotten socks, dirty dishes, cranky in-laws, bad credit, unemployment, sexual anxiety and dissatisfaction, and so on.

Let's not kid ourselves: Once we take off the artificial armor of chemical dependency, everything in our lives doesn't automatically get better. We don't suddenly know all the answers or even all the questions. Showing our real selves to the people we love may still be difficult.

Intimacy: A Definition

> *intimacy* (in'te-me-cē) n. 1. close or confidential association. 2. deeply personal, closely connected friendship. 3. pertaining to innermost feelings and thoughts. 4. sexual relations. 5. bound by strong affection, loyalty.

Intimacy is much more than love. Intimacy is a feeling of deep closeness and understanding between two people. It is trust, loyalty, friendship, sharing. An intimate relationship between a man and a woman will usually include sex. But not all sexual relationships are intimate. We can be desperately in love without sharing a trace of emotional closeness with our lover. For many people, life's harshest loneliness comes from loving a partner who doesn't seem to care. Without an emotional connection — without mutual caring — a relationship will become little more than an economic or sexual trade-off. A practical trade, perhaps, and even a cordial one. But not very satisfying.

Emotional intimacy as a goal in marriage is a relatively new idea. In Victorian times, financial stability, social status, and respectability were often more important concerns than love or physical compatibility. Happiness, especially for women, was considered an unnecessary luxury. Historian Mary S. Hartman wrote in *Victorian Murderesses* that one popular marriage manual published for our great grandmothers in 1889 devoted nearly an entire section to the disappointments of marriage. The manual gave this "sage" advice to young wives:

> Perhaps you are unhappy; perhaps your heart is bursting. But do not look for consolation, even in the realm of ideas, if these are dangerous or if they can become sinful. Resign yourself. Lose yourself completely in your children.

Few of us today are willing to resign ourselves to inconsolable unhappiness. In the last twenty years, society has undergone a radical transformation. We expect more from life than our parents or grandparents dared to dream. We are no longer constricted by the stultifying roles assigned to the good wife and good husband of the past. Almost without noticing the change, we have developed heightened expectations for personal growth and happiness.

On one hand, rising expectations offer us hope for a better life. And hope is certainly a good thing. But high expectations can also lead to bitter disappointment. If you turn on a TV talk show or attend a workshop on human potential and hear that the possibilities for human happiness and achievement are unlimited, you can come away feeling like a total failure if your own life doesn't measure up to the media ideal.

Now, listen: It's quite normal to yearn for that media ideal. And if we're normal we'll want more than personal recognition, more than just important work that contributes to society. In the process of fulfilling ourselves we will also hope to find a great love to give our lives meaning. After all, ever since childhood we've repeatedly heard that it's romantic love that makes the world go 'round.

Unfortunately, chemical dependency casts a dark shadow over our ability to develop satisfying love relationships. So, because our intimate lives are so messy and unsatisfying, we may end up labeling ourselves as neurotic losers, or as a man who can't love, or as a woman who loves too much.

Stop and consider this idea for a moment: *Chemical dependency, by its very nature, suffocates intimacy.*

Yes, that's right. If your life has been conflicted by chemical dependency — if you are a recovering addict, or the spouse of an addict, or the son or daughter of an addict — and if you are having trouble in your intimate relationships, then you're probably pretty normal. You are reacting as most other people who have found themselves in similar circumstances have reacted.

If your romantic life is in shambles and disarray, don't waste any more time beating yourself over the head and labeling yourself as sick or neurotic. Yes, you may feel fearful, defensive, angry, or emotionally burned-out. Yes, you're troubled and unhappy.

Get this clear: *Everyone* who spends any length of time involved in a chemically dependent relationship ends up feeling that way. Why should you be any different?

You see, chemical dependency makes people blind, deaf, and stupid. Before recovery, our daily lives are so consumed with crisis management that we can't hear our own voices or see our own behavior. We can't think straight or analyze our situation properly.

But with recovery comes the possibility of new awareness. For the first time we have the opportunity to examine the full range of factors working in our lives. And if you are at all like other survivors of chemical dependency, deceit has been a major factor in your life.

Living in an Atmosphere of Deception

Chemical dependency thrives on dishonesty, self-righteousness, and selfishness. It distorts our higher values, confuses us, turns us into liars and worse. The addict has to lie to protect his or her addiction from detection. And the spouse and child of an alcoholic or other drug abuser learns to lie and deny their true emotions too. It's all part of what we do to survive.

Let's face hard facts: *Deceit and emotional dishonesty are an integral part of chemical dependency* — for the addict, for the addict's spouse, and for the child who grows up in this atmosphere of deception. Our habits of emotional dishonesty are so ingrained that they're hard to break even after we begin the process of recovery. Unless we work hard at changing, deception will continue to follow us around like our own shadow.

Now here's another strange fact: *Most people whose lives have been conflicted by chemical dependency are basically honest and truth-loving.* That's right! We believe in honesty, yet we fib, prevaricate, cover up, deny, distort, delude, cheat, misrepresent, stretch the truth, tell tales, and just plain lie.

All this deception plays hell with our self-esteem, for there's no creature on earth more full of self-loathing, guilt, and fear than an honest liar. How can we possibly like and respect ourselves when our daily behavior violates our higher values? And how can we respect the people we love when we suspect they are deceiving us?

The sexual deception that Jack and Audrey perpetrated on each other is a classic example of the kind of behavior that destroys mutual love and self-respect. In the days of their courtship and young married life, sex had been exciting and satisfying for both of them. But as often happens, the excitement wore off. Their lovemaking deteriorated into a quick mechanical act which left both of them feeling vaguely cheated. Jack's chemical dependency made the situation worse. When he came home drunk, he was demanding, clumsy, and insensitive. The smell of him sickened Audrey. And when the alcohol made him impotent, he furiously accused her of not being woman enough to arouse him.

After Jack got sober and straight, his lovemaking improved, but sexual satisfaction still eluded Audrey. In a gentle manner, she asked Jack for a few minutes more foreplay during lovemaking. She explained that if he entered her before she was totally aroused, she failed to climax during intercourse.

Jack interpreted Audrey's request as a direct criticism of his manhood. He felt as if he'd been punched in the solar plexus. He was humiliated and angry and defiant. But he didn't talk about his feelings. He sulked and made cutting comments. When Audrey prodded him to talk about his feelings, he lied, saying nothing was wrong. His punishing attitude made life so miserable for Audrey, she gave up on the idea of having satisfying sex with her husband. Their sex life became a charade.

During lovemaking, Audrey moaned, gasped, and writhed with ladylike vigor, timing her little cries of pleasure to encourage Jack to hurry up and get it over with. Most of the time he was taken in by her faked orgasms, but not always. His sexual defensiveness grew. As did Audrey's anger. She hated herself for playing this stupid game, and she hated Jack for being so dense and insensitive.

Beating the Blame Game

Both Jack and Audrey found themselves bound up in a web of guilt and blame. Jack knew his wife was unhappy. This realization reinforced his sense of inadequacy and filled him with guilt. But instead of taking his own inventory — looking at his role in the problem — he started blaming all their marital difficulties on Audrey's unreasonable demands.

Looking back now, he's embarrassed by his attitude. "I was like a big baby," he admits. "I know now that a lot of alcoholics have ego problems, but I think I took the cake for stinking thinking. The idea that Audrey's pleasure was just as important as mine never occurred to me. I always put my needs first and I expected her to always put me first too. I wanted her to climax like skyrockets during sex to prove what a great lover I was. I just never realized how obnoxious my attitude was."

With the help of a counselor, Jack started making an effort to change. He wanted their marriage to work. But when he tried to talk about his new feelings with Audrey, she would have none of it! She no longer trusted her husband or his motives.

"When I married Jack," Audrey explains, "I was a trusting

and open person. I guess you could call me naive. But over the years I became bitter and disillusioned. I felt as if I was carrying the entire emotional responsibility for making our relationship work. When I tried to talk to Jack, he'd turn a cold shoulder to me or he'd make a sarcastic comment which put an end to the conversation. The implied threat was if I complained too much or if I put too many demands on the relationship, he'd stop loving me. I was always afraid of being abandoned, so I swallowed my rage. I was like a pretty little glass figurine filled with vile green poison. I loved Jack and I hated him. I blamed him for ruining my life and I was desperately afraid of losing him. I wanted him to die and I was afraid to let him out of my sight because something bad might happen to him. I couldn't think about anything but him and me and how much being married to him hurt."

But when Jack took the initiative in trying to improve their marriage, instead of being pleased, Audrey was furious. "After ten years of walking all over me, he makes a few efforts to be Mr. Nice Guy and he expects me to fall all over him in gratitude. That enraged me! What kind of patsy did he think I was? I wanted to punish him for all the pain he'd caused me. I wanted to see him squirm!"

Jack and Audrey finally separated. Divorce seemed inevitable. As a last resort they agreed to marriage counseling. Both Jack and Audrey went into counseling feeling like aggrieved victims. Audrey considered Jack to be an insensitive jerk and Jack thought his wife was a demanding bitch. In counseling they discovered they were no better, no worse than most other people. If one of them had been a *really* terrible person, divorce would probably have been the only solution.

Let's pause here for a minute. Could you be a little bit like Jack or Audrey? No better, no worse than most people? If you're a really terrible person, or if you are involved with a really terrible person, this book probably can't help you. But if you happen to be a fairly decent person who wants to learn how to give and receive love in a healthy way, perhaps this book can be of help. Let's do a short attitude and flexibility check:

- Are you willing to admit you have been less than perfectly honest and forthright in your intimate relationships?
- Are you willing to consider the possibility there have been times when your behavior was unfair, demanding, or selfish?
- Are you willing to concede your own personal act could use a little polish?
- Are you willing to take responsibility for your own life and well-being?

If you answered yes to each of those questions, then maybe you're ready for intimate recovery. But there's one more important test: *Are you ready to work on your own recovery, rather than expending your energies in an effort to change your partner?*

One of the enduring truths of recovery is that the only person we can truly change is ourself. So that's where we need to focus our attention: On ourselves.

Now, you may be saying, "Yes, I can see that, but how can I develop a loving and intimate relationship if my partner doesn't stop being such an insensitive, demanding jerk?"

That's a good question. For which we have no pat answer.

Our experience suggests that there can be love after addiction. While it takes two people to form an intimate partnership, it only takes one person to *start* the process of intimate recovery. For each of us, *the starting point is an internal decision to be more open, honest, and loving.* Until that decision is made, nothing else will change.

Thus we arrive at the key question: How do we get ourselves to open up and be honest, to make that internal decision to change, and to develop our capacity for love?

CHAPTER TWO

Barrier #1: Active Chemical Dependency or Codependency

Chemical dependency tears families and friendships apart and always — *always* — impairs the ability to develop open and honest intimate relationships. That's a hard and unpleasant fact.

Even so, there's good news: *Each person whose life has been adversely affected by alcohol and other drug abuse can experience intimate recovery.* This includes the addict, the addict's spouse, adult children of alcoholics, and even the parents of an addicted person. But in early recovery, intimacy issues are not at the top of the agenda. Intimacy issues come later, after we've dealt with the urgency of becoming drug-free.

First Things First

"Intimacy?" Inez laughs, shaking her head. "All through the years of Harold's heavy drinking — lost jobs, sudden relocations, making excuses to the boss when Harold was too hungover to get to work — I didn't have much time to spend on worrying about the lack of intimacy in our marriage. I was running a kind of a one-woman crisis clinic at home, trying to do as much damage control as possible. Paying the bills and dealing with creditors. Taking care of the kids. Running a typing service part-time out of my home. Of course, I felt there was probably a better way to live. I felt lonely and unloved. But so did everyone else I knew. I just tried to make the best of a bad situation."

After Harold went through treatment, intimacy issues began to surface. Inez recalls, "Gradually things began to change — it's hard to say exactly how. We spent more time together. Sober time, that is. Time when he was alert and listening. Got that? — *listening*. Sometimes I think listening may be the single most important act of intimacy. Really listening. That meant there was more time when I wasn't feeling oppressed and resentful. It wasn't a honeymoon by any means, but it was better by far than the way we had been."

Do Inez and Harold have any advice about overcoming barriers to intimacy?

Inez: "Yeah. First things first. Get the alcohol and other drugs out of your lives and then at least you'll be able to deal with the confusion with a clear head."

Harold: "It may take a while, but it's worth it."

Overcoming the Chemical Dependency Barrier

Before we continue, let's take time to ponder two questions:
1. *Has your life become unmanageable because of alcohol or other drugs?*

If so, and you are continuing to use alcohol or other drugs in any quantity, then you are still actively chemically dependent. Here are some common reactions when the issue of continued alcohol or other drug used is raised:

"But I only smoke dope on weekends."

"Hey, I just do a line now and then for recreational purposes, you know."

"I know I can't handle the hard stuff, so now I only drink beer."

These and other common strategies and rationalizations don't make our lives more manageable. They merely prolong our misery.

In this book, we take a hard line: If you want to improve

your life, *your first priority must be getting sober and straight.* Cutting down or switching from one drug to another turns out to be just one more act of self-deception, sham, and dishonesty.

2. *If you are not chemically dependent yourself, do you love someone who is?*

If so, you have a difficult task ahead. Just as addicts are obsessed with and dependent upon their drugs of choice, those closest to the addict — friends, parents, lover — may become obsessed with trying to control and take care of the addict. It's an overwhelming task, inevitably marked by frustration and futility. Preoccupied with trying to control and change the people we love, we end up losing control over our own health and well-being.

Coping with Codependency

Many therapists see this obsession to control as a sign of *codependency.* Codependent people often appear strong and self-possessed on the surface. But the appearance masks a grim reality. Scratch the shiny veneer of our apparent strength and poise, and a different creature emerges. Regardless of social status or accomplishments in life, we frequently feel weak, insecure, and incompetent.

Just who and what are we?

That question baffles us. One codependent wife described her confusion: "One moment I feel like the grandest, most deserving, most powerful person in the universe. A few small disappointments later and I feel like a dish of rancid dog food."

This seesaw in identity is one of the most compelling factors in our obsessive need to control the behavior and feelings of the people around us. Because we look to other people for validation and approval, we are almost always on a collision course with somebody or something. We truly believe if we can only get the other people in our lives to act the way we want them to, then everybody will be happy. Even though our motives may be good — all we want is to make things work out right — our behavior is ultimately destructive and unloving.

It's almost impossible to be closely involved with an alcoholic or other drug addict for any length of time and not develop symptoms of codependency. Why? Partly because emotionally unhealthy people are attracted to other unhealthy people. And as a rule, healthy, stable people seek out other healthy people.

What does this mean in practical terms? If a relationship is to continue, either the addict has to get as emotionally stable as the healthy partner, or the healthy partner has to get as emotionally sick as the addict.

People who possess the emotional strength to resist the pull of codependency won't allow themselves to be sucked into the addict's distorted version of reality. They'll recognize strange, weird, destructive behavior when they see it and they won't feel any need to make up excuses to explain away the screaming evidence that something is terribly wrong. Usually they'll offer some kind of useful advice, like, "For God's sake, get some treatment." And if their help is rejected, they'll detach themselves from the sick relationship.

People with high self-esteem and a strong sense of identity usually believe they deserve to be treated with dignity and respect. They won't put up with the lies, abuse, and craziness that accompany chemical dependency. In contrast, the codependent person deals with the craziness by merging with it.

Warning: Don't Merge with the Craziness

When Dean looks back, he can see how he got sucked into the craziness of his wife's addiction. He's a probation officer who appears to be the essence of tough competence at work. He doesn't take any nonsense when it comes to the pathetic excuses of his probationers. He can see through lies and evasions and flimflam with the sharp insight that years of experience have given him. Yet, when Dean's alcoholic wife, Violet, backed her car into a neighbor's pickup truck, Dean covered up for her. When she wrote bad checks, he made them good. When she clawed his face in a drunken rage, Dean threw her against a wall, then, shocked by his violence, he cried and apologized for hurting her.

As Violet's behavior became increasingly more bizarre and erratic, Dean worked harder and harder not to antagonize her. He refused all social engagements, especially with people from work. He made excuses. He lied. When family and friends made comments about Violet's moodiness and sickly appearance, Dean explained, "Violet's depressed because her career isn't going the way she'd like." He didn't tell anyone that Violet's career had stalled because she was too unreliable and unstable to maintain a steady job.

Dean mistakenly believed that as long as he provided enough money, structure, and support, Violet would eventually see the light and change. At a minimum, he felt he could keep Violet's drinking and wild spending sprees under reasonable control.

Of course, he was wrong. Violet's addiction progressed, their marriage deteriorated, and Dean found himself in trouble at work because he was spending more time dealing with Violet than with his job. He was tired, distracted, and irritable with his co-workers. His colleagues no longer respected him. In the end, he had merged his own identity with the craziness that went with his wife's addictive disease.

If, like Dean, you are (or have been) deeply involved in a relationship with a chemically dependent person, don't merge with the craziness. Make this your first priority: *Stop focusing your attention and energy on controlling the mismanaged life of your partner and start working on your own mismanaged life.*

Addiction and Intimacy: Love on the Rocks

It is absolutely essential that we recognize the widely destructive effect active addiction and codependency have on our intimate lives. Chemical dependency and codependency crush us physically, emotionally, and spiritually. We cannot be addicted — and we cannot love a person who is addicted — and escape unscathed. But once we accept and understand the many ways that chemical dependency makes us prisoners to emotional pain, we can take concrete steps to liberate ourselves.

Freedom from chemical dependency then gives us the opportunity to make our intimate relationships more satisfying and fulfilling.

> *First, we must understand that it is impossible to have a satisfying intimate relationship with a person who is actively chemically dependent.*

True, there may be wistful moments of intimacy, moments of deep and tender sharing. But they are unpredictable. Addicted partners are unreliable — they can't be counted on. More: The kind of intimacy that occurs in drug-affected relationships is a sham intimacy, a pseudo-intimacy that has the form and sometimes the outward trappings of intimacy, but remains shallow and superficial.

This means that if you are abusing alcohol or other drugs, or if you are *involved with* someone who is, you are deceiving yourself if you are trying to improve your love life while ignoring the addiction.

Addiction distorts our thinking processes in such a way that we inevitably become untrustworthy. Our behavior becomes more self-centered and dishonest. Addiction is a major barrier to intimacy because we cannot be consistently honest and unselfish. We may make sincere efforts to be a loving partner but our continued use of alcohol and other drugs, or our efforts to cover up for a chemically dependent partner, will always sabotage these good intentions.

Now we have reached the point where a great many of us hit a brick wall — our partner steadfastly refuses to change, refuses to cooperate, and frequently refuses to discuss the alcohol or drug problem.

Don't despair. Each of us, individually, can start the process of becoming a more open, honest, and loving person, even when our partner remains stuck in addiction or codependency.

Why Treatment is Necessary

It's been said that the road to hell is paved with good intentions. Certainly in the realm of chemical dependency, there is no shortage of good intentions. But good intentions soon wear thin unless they are followed by consistently good behavior.

Consider John and Linda, married for fifteen years. If asked about their relationship, John would insist that he truly loves his wife. "Of course, I love her. What kind of question is that?" He'd be insulted if anyone asked if he wanted to be a good husband. "I *am* a good husband. I mean, most of the time. I try. I mean, it comes with the territory."

But when John drinks, he becomes totally unreliable. He stops off with his buddies for a drink after work, fully intending to be home in time for dinner. Somehow one drink leads to two, then three, and pretty soon it's midnight. Anticipating his wife's anger, he makes up stories to explain his behavior and he lies about how much money he spends. Of course, he always promises it won't happen again. But it does, again and again. Linda, tired of his lies and promises, threatens divorce. John sweet-talks her and goes on his good behavior for a week or two.

When Linda recently reached the breaking point and turned her threat of divorce into a reality, John was baffled. "I don't know what happened. It came out of nowhere. One day we were getting along just fine, then the next thing I know I'm served with divorce papers and evicted from my own house." After a few scotch-and-waters, he glumly complains, "How could she do that to me? I loved her, I always loved her. Didn't that count for anything? Now I can't even talk with her without her lawyer being present. What the hell was going on all those years we were together? What the hell did she want?"

Active addicts and codependents can love passionately, but not wholeheartedly. John's love for Linda seemed real — in the sense that he truly believed his own words when he said, "I love you, I need you." But his addiction had become more powerful than his good intentions. He couldn't see his selfishness. His repeated passionate declarations of love sounded to Linda like a set of nice-sounding phrases trotted out on cue whenever he got in trouble.

If we are like John, we can love with a desperate intensity, but we cannot wholly commit ourselves to another person because we are in bondage to our addiction. Addiction is a desperate and selfish illness, and it creates only desperate and selfish love.

These are harsh words, words we may not want to hear. Nonetheless, they are true. Chemical dependency is the Great Destroyer of human relationships. It dominates every aspect of our lives, alienating us from our higher values and stripping us of our integrity.

Recovery can put us back in touch with our higher values, enabling us to give and receive love in an honest and caring way.

The Beginnings of Intimate Recovery

When it comes to intimate recovery, addicts and codependents face identical tasks. *There are no significant differences between us.* Each of us has been both victim and victimizer.

Some people find these assertions shocking, even offensive. "I'm not the one who passed out on the floor in my own vomit," Janet told her counselor. "I'm not the one who took the money out of the kids' savings accounts. I'm the one who's been holding this family together." She added indignantly, "*I* don't need to change. My husband does."

Janet's feelings are understandable. For the past ten years she'd been coping with the chaos created by her husband's alcoholism. Gary's drinking, temper tantrums, and irresponsibility had been a part of daily life.

In contrast, Janet had behaved responsibly. She was the one who had dealt with angry creditors, unhappy children, and critical relatives.

Gary was finally in treatment, and Janet was happy about that, but she didn't like some of the things the counselors were saying. She had come to the treatment center to help Gary. So where did this counselor get off telling her she had to start her own recovery program? Yes, she was upset and unhappy. *But,* Janet reasoned, *my problems are a direct result of Gary's drinking.* Gary was the addict. Gary was the patient. Gary was the one who needed a recovery program. Not Janet.

Whose Responsibility Is It?

Janet's reasoning is faulty. She needs a recovery program just as much as Gary does because over the years she's developed a number of resentments and fears. There's no question that her husband behaved badly. He lied, he intimidated her physically and emotionally, he squandered money, and he was sexually unfaithful. There were moments when Janet hated him, moments when she even wished him dead. She feels cheated by life, despairing, anxious, and distrustful.

These feelings interfere with her ability to love, work, and form friendships. Her life has been so stressful, so full of turbulence and uncertainty that at times she feels like a ticking time bomb primed to explode. In short, living with Gary's chemical dependency has made her own life unmanageable.

Gary's sobriety will not eliminate Janet's resentments and dissatisfaction. Ten years ago, her anger may have been a momentary reaction to external circumstances. No more. Her anger, bitterness, and negativity have now become a deeply ingrained and habitual way of responding to life.

Just as Gary must confront his addiction and make corrections and amends, Janet must confront her own pain and anger. Instead of putting her energy into "helping" Gary's recovery, she must stop holding him responsible for her happiness and take charge of her own life. Only then will she be free to give and receive the love she so desperately desires.

For each of us, addict and codependent alike, recovery begins when we stop holding other people responsible for our problems. Blame provides comforting excuses, but blame never changes circumstances. It may momentarily make us feel better to blame someone else for our deep unhappiness, but blame does nothing to help us change our behavior. *Blame leaves everything the same.*

"But I was hurt and betrayed by my husband."
"My wife's addiction to cocaine tore our whole family apart."
"His boozing created havoc in our lives."
"Her nerve pills turned her into a zombie."

Yes, we've been hurt and betrayed by others, but we'll never get better if we sit around waiting for somebody else to change in order to make us happy.

A Drug-Free Atmosphere for Intimacy

Pause here a moment and ask yourself some questions:

- Are you willing to admit that your life is unmanageable?
- Are you willing to stop holding other people responsible for your feelings and happiness?
- Are you willing to concentrate on changing yourself instead of other people?

If you answered yes to all three questions, you are on the threshold of recovery. Here's one more important question:

- Regardless of your past history of alcohol and other drug use, are you willing to become abstinent?

Abstinence from alcohol and other drugs is a basic requirement of intimate recovery for *both the addict and the codependent.*

While we all recognize the importance of abstinence for alcoholics and other drug addicts, many codependents see abstinence for themselves as highly unfair. "I'm not the addict," they protest. "Why should I have to give up something that gives me pleasure just because my partner can't handle it?"

There are three reasons why codependent partners may balk at the idea of abstinence for themselves.

Reason #1: The codependent partner is protecting someone who has an unidentified or hidden chemical dependency problem.

Reason #2: The codependent partner is consciously or unconsciously attempting to sabotage the recovery of the addict.

Reason #3: Both of the above.

These are all bad reasons.

Abstinence alone is not the ultimate answer to all our problems. It's merely the starting point, the place from which we begin our journey toward intimate recovery.

Think of it this way: When you choose abstinence you make a powerful statement of love. You are saying, "I care enough about myself to stop contributing to my own destruction." And you are also telling the people you love, "I care enough about you to stop contributing to your destruction."

While it is true that we can only change ourselves, it is equally true that we can create the kind of loving atmosphere that invites positive change in the people around us. Recovery does not automatically restore intimacy, but for those of us who have been hurt by chemical dependency, a life free from alcohol and other drugs is the first step in overcoming all the other barriers to intimacy. It is an honest and clear statement to the world, saying, "I care!"

CHAPTER THREE

Barrier #2: Lack of Honest Self-Knowledge

Mirror, Mirror on the Wall

Justin considers himself an honest person, and in many ways he is. "Look," Justin says, "I've got — what? — a year, thirteen months, in the program. I can look at myself in the mirror when I get up. That's the key to recovery. Honesty. You've gotta be able to look at yourself in the mirror."

But do we always see the truth in the mirror? Sometimes the truth hurts, especially when it tells a story we don't want to hear. It's common for us to pay attention only to the truths we like while we ignore the unpleasant truths that have the power to make us feel bad about ourselves. Not only can we deceive and mislead others, we often deceive ourselves. We can conveniently compartmentalize our lives, acknowledging only the little boxes of behavior that make us look like heroes.

Justin would no more steal, lie to a client, or cheat a co-worker than he would drink his morning coffee with a shot of shaving lotion. But he lies to his girlfriends all the time. If he wants sex, he'll tell the woman he's with that he loves her, then he'll never call her again. Justin will lead a woman on, making her believe he's ready for commitment, then he'll disappear without an explanation. And when he finds a woman he really likes, Justin will demand her complete loyalty and faithfulness while he continues to play the field.

How does he justify his outrageous behavior? "When I'm dating a woman," Justin explains, "I never promise I'll be exclusive, I never say I won't see other women. But I know most women get upset if a guy they're sleeping with goes out with someone else, so I lie to keep from hurting anybody's feelings. Look, I'm not exactly seducing virgins, you know. The women I date are old enough to know the score. It's just that women have this thing — you spend some time with them and they start acting as if you promised them something, and I end up going along with it so as not to hurt them. But, really, I don't think it's my job to meet other people's expectations. I've never forced anyone to go to bed with me. If they want to put more meaning in it than I do, that's their problem, not mine."

Integrity Lapses

In his business dealings, Justin plays by the proper rules.

- He doesn't lie.
- He doesn't cheat.
- He doesn't steal.
- He doesn't exploit others for his own selfish gain.

But in his intimate life, it's strictly "Buyer Beware." Can a person really call himself honest if his integrity only shines through when it's convenient? Why is it wrong to run a scam on a business acquaintance, but all right to do it to a lover? When talking objectively about his love and sex life, Justin admits that he's not always straightforward and sincere. But he has a ready explanation to make it all right in his own mind: "I just let the women in my life believe what they want to believe. That's not so bad, is it? Not when you consider I do it to avoid hurting their feelings."

Here's another point of view: Justin lies to avoid the *natural consequences* of his selfish behavior — he lies to avoid the natural anger and rejection that would come from the women he uses if they knew his real motives, his real intentions. The truth hurts, and Justin has a gut-level feeling that if he told the truth and got rejected, he might be the one who would hurt the most.

What would it be like if Justin told the truth? What would happen if he looked soulfully into the eyes of his date and told her, "Hey, I'm not really interested in getting to know you very well. I'm only interested in my needs. Don't expect anything from this relationship. I go to bed with a lot of women. I'd like to get you in bed tonight, no strings attached, just a pleasant interlude. We might see each other again, but probably not. But what the hell, we're both adults. We both have needs. I respect your independence too much to even talk about commitment. If you get hurt, well, it's your tough luck."

A healthy response would be: "I'm glad you warned me. Thanks for the cup of coffee. See you later, big guy."

While Justin prides himself on living an honest program of recovery, his behavior shows that in the area of intimacy, he continues to be selfish and dishonest.

The Value of Confusion

Intimacy does not mean that we should sacrifice all our own interests. But it does require something much more and different from a "me first" or "you first" attitude. Just as there are ethical rules for running a business, there are ethical rules for intimacy. Clear rules, demanding rules. The basic rule is this: *We act not only in our own self-interest, but also in the interest of others.* Such a rule precludes both rampant selfishness and unending self-sacrifice. In intimate recovery, the goal is to have things work out well for ourselves *and* for our partner.

"But I get confused," Justin says. "Sometimes I don't know what's right and what's wrong. I get scared. I don't know what the right answer is so I just follow my emotions."

None of us likes to admit that the way we conduct our intimate lives is defective. So we sometimes use our emotional confusion as an excuse.

"I'm so confused."
"I'm not ready to make a decision."
"I have problems in sorting things out."

Listen: There's no such thing as a recovering alcoholic, addict, codependent, or adult child who isn't confused some of the time. And while our confusion, our anger, and our fears are real, they do not legitimize dishonest and exploitive behavior. Of course our past traumas, psychological pain, and distressing emotions influence our behavior, but they don't justify dishonesty, selfishness, or meanness.

When it comes to relationships, there are many legitimate areas for confusion, areas where perhaps there are no "right" and "wrong" answers. Who handles the checkbook? Who does the dishes? Should a mother work or should she stay home with the kids? Or should the father be a house husband? What's the best sexual position? These are open questions that couples must answer according to their particular beliefs and needs. What's right and appropriate for one couple may be completely unworkable for another couple with different needs.

So, yes, there is a lot of room for confusion, a lot of gray areas where recovering men and women must work hard to decide what is right for them as individuals and as a couple. But in our culture we also operate under a clear-cut set of rules and expectations that define on the most basic level what is acceptable behavior. These rules are part of our national character, part of the fabric of our lives, woven throughout our history, our literature, our folklore, movies, television, and newscasts.

The rules are clear and simple. We all know them even when we choose to ignore them. We're not supposed to go around lying and sneaking. We're not supposed to break promises. We're not supposed to physically abuse or emotionally terrorize people. We're not supposed to exploit the vulnerable nor betray the trusting. We're not supposed to demean, ridicule, or humiliate the people we love. We're supposed to be fair.

This is basic stuff. It's so elemental and corny that we sometimes forget the powerful hold these simple doctrines have on our lives. Yet, when these doctrines are violated, we respond immediately, with outrage. Our response does not come from the intellect, it comes from the guts. When victimized, lied to, cheated, or betrayed, righteous anger engulfs us. And when we are the liar and the sneak, we feel shame, guilt, and self-hate.

Chemical dependency and codependency force people into breaking the basic cultural rules we use to define who is a decent person. It doesn't matter if we have ever talked about the rules, or written them down, "Rule One . . . Rule Two. . . " and so on. They are something we just know. If we continue to violate these basic rules, we cannot possibly like and respect ourselves. And if we dislike ourselves, we cannot experience the love and freedom of genuine intimacy.

I'm Okay, You're Flawed

When we hurt other people, we don't want to admit it. When we're selfish, we don't want to hear about it. When we're scared, we want to ignore it. We deceive, we demand, we push, and we pull. We get our feelings hurt, we get mad, and so do the people we're dealing with. Pretty soon, everything's a big mess. That, in a nutshell, describes behavior among chemically dependent people. It's a barren ground for intimacy.

Of course, we want an explanation for why our lives are such a big mess. Because we don't want to feel like we're always the one who messes everything up, we need an explanation that makes the recurring problems in our lives not our fault. The process goes something like this:

1. We find ourselves in a bad situation. (Take your pick, there are thousands to choose from.)
2. We experience distressing emotions, physical pain and

hardship, or both.
3. We decide we have to do something to stop our distress, and we see two choices:
   a. assume responsibility for our lives, and start the hard job of doing whatever it takes to get well and healthy.
   b. blame others for our problems and demand that they change before we do.

Now, if we choose option "b" — if we cope with our problems by blaming others for our pain — our task becomes fairly simple. You see, one of life's enduring truths is that no one is perfect. Therefore, we can *always* find some inconsiderate, unfair, or horrible thing that somebody else did to us. We can look around and easily come up with a big list of wrongs committed against us.

Our next step is to shift the responsibility for our pain off our shoulders and dump it onto the people and situations on our list. Our problems become *their* fault.

Great! And if it's their fault, then we must be blameless. In our minds we become innocent victims, trapped by our pain until those other bad people start acting right.

Peter's Story

Once we decide to play the victim's role, our egos start playing all kinds of tricks on our minds. Only those ideas, thoughts, and beliefs that already fit with our distorted perceptions of the world are allowed to enter our consciousness. Our egos color our perceptions until what we see has little to do with reality.

Consider Peter's recent ordeal. Peter's been sober and straight for almost a year. But after completing an intensive inpatient treatment program, he ignored his counselor's advice about attending aftercare and recovery meetings. Peter chose to go it alone. He and his current girlfriend, Sukie, have been dating for six months and have talked vaguely of getting married.

Due to complications from a ruptured appendix, Peter was in the hospital for three weeks. Sukie drove forty miles round-trip to visit him every day. She took care of his dog, collected his mail, paid his bills, brought him books and magazines and candy. Then one day, toward the end of his stay, Sukie's six-year-old daughter came down with a serious ear infection. What could she do? She had to choose between visiting Peter in the hospital or taking care of her child. She called Peter and explained she couldn't visit him for a couple of days.

Peter was furious.

Even though he was almost totally recovered from his illness and was receiving top-notch medical care, he felt betrayed and abandoned. His all-consuming ego demanded that Sukie put his needs and desires above all else. In reality, Sukie had been attentive, considerate, and loving. But in Peter's mind, she had selfishly deserted him in his hour of greatest need. His bloated ego prevented him from seeing the loving and kind things Sukie had done for him. All he could see was his own loneliness, boredom, and resentment.

His ordeal was what counted, *his* feelings, *his* needs. *After all,* Peter thought, *I'm the one who's hurt.*

The Tyranny of the Ego

Peter believed that Sukie should always put him first, no matter what. Even though this belief was unreasonable and childish, it colored all of his actions. When she came to visit him again after a two day absence, he was sarcastic and mean to her. But he felt justified. *I'm just giving her what she deserves,* he told himself. *She'll think twice before she dumps on me again.*

Sukie left in tears, biting her tongue to hold back the angry words she longed to say. "Peter scares me when he gets like that," Sukie later told a friend. "So I give in. It's the classic situation where the man gets abusive and the woman shuts up and tries to make nice. I apologized and promised it wouldn't happen again, but I'm so mad. Doesn't he see how unfair he's being? I'm doing the best I can, but it never seems to be enough to please him. Sometimes I think that as soon as he gets back on his feet, I should just break the whole thing off. But I can't do it now, not while he's down. Besides, I think I still love him."

In this kind of atmosphere, true emotional intimacy is impossible. There can be no meeting of minds and certainly no meeting of hearts. Peter is an angry tyrant and Sukie is an angry doormat. Though their love for each other is still there, it's quickly becoming an accumulation of conflicting demands and resentments, not a sharing of their true selves.

Both Sukie and Peter have work to do if their love is to become a source of pleasure. Peter's attitudes are selfish and immature.

As *Alcoholics Anonymous*, or The Big Book, points out:

Selfishness — self-centeredness! That, we think, is the root of our troubles. Driven by a hundred forms of fear, self-delusion, self-seeking, and self-pity, we step on the toes of our fellows and they retaliate. Sometimes they hurt us, seemingly without provocation, but we invariably find that at some time in the past we have made decisions based on self which later placed us in a position to be hurt.

So our troubles, we think, are basically of our own making. They arise out of ourselves, and the alcoholic is an extreme example of self-will run riot, though he usually doesn't think so. Above everything, we alcoholics must be rid of this selfishness. We must, or it kills us!

Sukie, too, could benefit from taking a closer look at her behavior. While it is true that she has done her best to please Peter and in return he has treated her badly, she has *allowed* it to happen. Since they first met, she has made a habit of giving in to Peter's aggression. (She allowed her former husband to abuse her too.) Never once has she drawn the line. Never has she said, "Stop it! I'm not going to let you treat me this way."

Because Sukie fears being alone and having to be financially and emotionally responsible for herself, she gives men the power to treat her badly. She also doesn't want to be considered bitchy or a bad woman, so instead of openly standing up for herself (which she considers unfeminine) she connives and manipulates behind Peter's back in order to get what she needs and wants from him.

The Intimate Inventory

Alcoholics Anonymous tells us that an essential part of any recovery program is the Fourth Step, *a searching and fearless moral inventory of ourselves.* Taking a moral inventory means removing the distorting lens of our all-consuming ego, removing the false beliefs which bring us so much pain.

The Big Book sets forth the Fourth Step in a nutshell: "We took stock honestly. First, we searched out the flaws in our makeup which caused our failure. Being convinced that self, manifested in various ways, was what had defeated us, we considered its common manifestations."

Some of the common manifestations of "self" include:

- *Resentments*: Bad feelings toward others who we think have wronged us. Jealous grudges against those who we think have had good fortune they clearly don't deserve. A bitter mind-set.
- *Fear*: We're afraid we'll be found out, afraid of changes in routine, afraid we'll be humiliated or embarrassed.
- *Shame*: The sense that we've done something very wrong, something we can never overcome or atone for.
- *Dishonesty*: Lies, damn lies, and statistics. Petty deceptions and whoppers.

- *Closed-mindedness*: There is only one right way.
- *Self-righteousness*: The only right way is *my* way.
- *Self-centeredness*: I did it my way — and everyone should notice how remarkable I am.
- *Self-pity*: Nobody loves me and my hands are cold.
- *Self-aggrandizement*: I am accomplished beyond the dreams of ordinary mortals and favored in the sight of God.
- *Selfish martyrdom*: I've suffered in life and people have treated me badly, but I'm a survivor, and I'll just go on suffering to everyone's awe at my great sacrifice.

For many of us, these feelings are most intense and troublesome in the areas of love, sex, and intimacy. That's why an *intimate inventory* — that is, taking stock of the ideas, beliefs, and actions that have affected our intimate lives — is an important part of our overall inventory.

While in chemical dependency treatment, Peter had spent several days taking his inventory. He examined his resentments and his misdeeds. He forgave those who had offended him and made amends to those he had hurt. It was a moving experience for him, and months later he was still using some of the knowledge he had gained.

But Peter made a grave mistake. He took his inventory while in treatment, then he stopped. *I'm glad that's out of the way,* he said to himself. Peter didn't realize that a personal inventory is *never* out of the way. Every day challenges us — every day something happens that riles our emotions, triggers anger, teases our fears. Each day has its disappointments, large and small. Every day something happens that tests our attitudes and values.

Peter's attitudes toward intimacy, love, sex, and women weren't a big issue while he was in treatment because he wasn't involved in a relationship then. His inventory barely touched on the subject of intimacy. But when he fell in love with Sukie, buried attitudes, fears, and desires came thundering to the surface. These needed examination, but Peter ignored them as much as possible.

His illness brought on another flood of emotion. Suddenly he was facing the prospect of helplessness, vulnerability, disability, even death. He found himself dependent on strangers for his care, and dependent on Sukie for love, support, and contact with the outside world. His dependency angered him, made him feel powerless, less than a man. And in his powerlessness and fear, he struck out at the person he loved and needed most — Sukie.

By failing to examine his feelings, thoughts, and attitudes, Peter sabotaged his intimate relationship with Sukie. Instead of looking inside himself, he struck out, driving a wedge between himself and the woman he loved. It was easier for him to blame Sukie for his emotional distress than it was to look at his own beliefs and fears. Peter was being dishonest, and he showed his dishonesty in different ways:

- It was easier to make sarcastic comments than it was to admit he felt powerless and dependent.
- It was easier to yell than to admit that he was lonely and frightened.
- It was easier to be aggressive and abusive toward a woman who was afraid to stand up to him than it was to face the prospect of his own vulnerability and mortality.

Don't Stop before the Job is Done

Peter is not an ignorant lout. He's an intelligent man, a man of intense feeling and sensitivity. He's worked hard to put his life together. He's searched and struggled, and made remarkable strides. Unfortunately, he stopped before the job was over.

Selfishness, fear, and anger are not temporary abnormalities we can work on for a few days, then put behind us. They are an ongoing part of the human condition. In moments of serenity, we may indeed feel that we have tamed the dragons inside our souls, but at the slightest sign of stress our dragons roar again. When we are frightened, angry, and lonely, the temptation to lie, blame, and punish is strongest. And that is exactly when our need for an ongoing inventory is strongest.

Peter learned this valuable lesson from a blunt-talking cleaning woman. She cleaned Peter's room every night and was often present while Sukie and Peter visited. "It's none of my business," the cleaning woman said, after watching Sukie leave the hospital in tears, "but, Peter, you're behaving like a horse's derriere. If a man talked to me the way you talk to that little girlfriend of yours, I'd let him lay in his hospital bed and rot. She loves you and you love her and you treat her like dirt. If you don't start working your program, son, you're heading for big trouble."

Peter was outraged at the woman's impertinence. Then she reached into her pocket and pulled out a medallion. She showed it to Peter. "Look familiar?" she asked.

Peter nodded.

The cleaning woman was a graduate of the same treatment program as Peter. "Want to talk?" she asked.

Peter felt himself choked with emotion. It was like a dam was bursting inside. He'd been running from the truth for months, and it had finally caught him.

With help and encouragement from others in recovery, Peter began examining his thoughts, attitudes, and feelings. Taking his cue from Chapter Five of *Alcoholics Anonymous*, he decided to examine his intimate behavior. The book instructed:

> We reviewed our own conduct over the years past. Where had we been selfish, dishonest, or inconsiderate? Whom had we hurt? Did we unjustifiably arouse jealousy, suspicion or bitterness? Where were we at fault, what should we have done instead? We got this all down on paper and looked at it.
>
> In this way we tried to shape a sane and sound ideal for our future sex life. We subjected each relation to this test — was it selfish or not?

Peter's inventory showed him that his relationship with Sukie had been riddled with selfishness and dishonesty. "I discovered I have a history of using women as emotional whipping posts. If I'm upset about something, I take it out on the woman in my life. If I had a bad day at work, I'd come home mad and pick a fight with Sukie. If I was worried or scared about something, I'd find some way to shift my thinking away from whatever my problem was and blame my bad feelings on something Sukie was doing. It was real simple — as long as I could find fault with Sukie, I didn't have to look at myself.

"There were also some times when I just plain out and out lied to Sukie, and there were a couple of one-night stands with other women. I justified this dishonest behavior by telling myself I wouldn't be acting that way if Sukie did a better job of meeting my needs. Which is pure baloney. Even if Sukie does something bad, that doesn't make it all right for me to be a liar. I had this illusion about myself, you see. I thought I was this real honest guy. When I lied and carried on like a jerk, it was always — in my own mind — because someone else was forcing me into it. It was their fault, not mine. Therefore, I was still the good guy. As soon as *they* shaped up, all my problems would be solved. The most painful part of my inventory was the realization that I wasn't always the guy in the white hat."

Becoming Honest with Care and Compromise

Sukie was so impressed with the change in Peter's attitude and behavior that she started reading his recovery literature. She, too, started working on her intimate inventory. "What a shock!" Sukie later admitted. "I've always tried to be Little Miss Sunshine, fixing up everybody's problems. I grew up thinking that as long as I was nice, people should be nice to me, that they should give me what I wanted. Well . . . it doesn't always work that way. I've been nice all over the place and I've waited and waited for my needs to be met in return and it just hasn't happened. I've been so hurt and disappointed by people I loved and trusted."

By taking her inventory Sukie came to realize that instead of being the kind and loving person she imagined herself to be, she was actually a bitter, negative, and angry woman.

"I refused to take any responsibility for my own feelings," Sukie now confesses. "I thought that if I knocked myself out trying to please a man, that in return he should take complete responsibility for making me happy. When that didn't happen, I felt totally betrayed. I was so angry! Here I was, picturing myself as Merry Sunshine when I was actually up to my eyeballs in hate."

Taking an intimate inventory is hard. Both Peter and Sukie had to face unpleasant truths. Both had to admit that while they operated with the best of intentions, their basic stance toward life was dishonest.

Peter — who thought of himself as the guy in the white hat — discovered that he was frequently selfish and demanding. Sukie — who thought of herself as loving and giving — discovered that she harbored intense resentments and a lot of hateful feelings toward people she loved.

The intimate inventory was the beginning of a positive change in Peter and Sukie's relationship. When they stopped being so blaming and resentful toward each other, they were able to feel a lot more love. But the problems weren't solved. Together they decided to see a therapist for premarital counseling. "Peter and I still argue," Sukie admits. "But slowly we're both learning to be more reasonable and less demanding. He's not so selfish and I'm not so self-sacrificing. We both give and we both take. We loved each other before . . . now we *care* about each other too. And, believe me, that's a major difference."

CHAPTER FOUR

Barrier #3: Communication Myths

Myth: Just Communicate

One widely advocated solution to intimacy problems is improved communication skills. The communication expert sees intimacy problems developing like this: The foundation of any relationship is communication. Partners misunderstand each other because they have not developed the proper communication skills. Small misunderstandings become major catastrophes when communication fails, spoiling the relationship and destroying intimacy.

Poor communication between partners is one very clear, very concrete, symptom when intimacy fails. So clear and concrete, in fact, that many folks believe better communication will remedy *all* problems of intimacy. Thus: Learn better communication skills, learn to express yourself clearly, learn to listen. Then it will all fall into place.

So far, so good. But the communication problem may be tougher to deal with than the obvious solution suggests.

Consider this: Chemical dependency impairs open and honest communication by making people who know how to express themselves afraid to open up. It makes smart people afraid to look at and listen to what's going on around them.

The key word here is *fear*. Stop and think about your experiences in a family or relationship complicated by chemical dependency. What were discussions like?

- Was there an easy and honest flow of communication? Or was talking to each other about thoughts, feelings, and plans dangerous?
- Were there times when you presented your ideas in a rational, loving, and open manner and your partner returned your efforts with indifference or rage?
- Were there times when your strung-out emotions meant you couldn't or wouldn't listen to a reasonable and clear expression from your partner?
- Did one person dominate every attempted discussion by being loud and argumentative, snide and sarcastic, or so obviously and aggravatingly *always right*?
- Was there a sense of unpredictability — with Mom and Dad (or your partner) being cordial and congenial at times, and then with little or no warning lapsing into sullen silences or unreasonable rages?
- Was television your best friend and confidante? Books? Poetry?

Not being heard and not being able to express ourselves to the people who are important to us can be terribly frustrating. Small worries, hurts, and fears can pile up, until we feel as though we might burst apart at the seams from internal pressure. Over and over we're told we must learn to express these feelings if we are to attain emotional health and intimacy.

When intimacy fails, the assumption is that the problem is caused by a lack of effective communication skills. The easy, pat solution is communication skill-building. But wait a minute! How many of us are *truly* lacking in communication skills? Yes, there are timid souls who find it impossible to utter a word. And we've all met aggressive loudmouths who are so obnoxious they chase everyone away. But most of us are capable of carrying on a conversation. We know how to listen, when to speak, when to pause, how to persuade, even how to be eloquent.

Here's an irony, then: David ignores his wife and grunts at his children, but his boss says, "Dave's a primo negotiator and a very skilled problem solver. He's an invaluable asset to our company." And Maria, a woman who constantly criticizes and nags her husband, is a source of inspiration and comfort to her women friends. What's going on here? Perhaps there's more investment in success on the job or in casual friendship than there is in a relationship gone sour. Perhaps it's not so scary to communicate with people who don't know our vulnerabilities, with people who we haven't lived with closely. David, after all, has not lived with the people he works with. Maria's friends see only a small slice of her life.

Many of us, including those who seem completely closed up, are painfully eager to express our deepest, most heartfelt feelings if only we can find a safe way to do it. Unfortunately, there are few places we can express honest emotion without risks, especially if our family or relationship is complicated by addiction. And because most of us still have our wits about us, *we choose not to use the communication skills we already possess* because we know there's a good chance we'll get clobbered emotionally or physically if we are honest and forthright.

Sarah's Dilemma

Recently, a friend named Sarah called us in tears. She had just finished reading a book on how recovering people can improve their marriages and families. According to the book, families scarred by chemical dependency can become happy, healthy, and nurturing if everyone — Mom, Dad, the kids, even the grandparents — cooperate and work together. The book outlined a sensible and seemingly simple path to family solidarity: Communicate more effectively. If family members would just learn to express their needs and feelings to their partners in a healthy and loving manner, then those needs and feelings would be honored.

How could this be accomplished? The authors suggested

families can be healed through family roundtable discussions or family problem-solving sessions.

Do the husband and wife have a hard time getting privacy? No problem. Just enlist the grandparents as occasional weekend babysitters so Mom and Dad can enjoy private romantic interludes together. Nothing could be simpler.

Not according to Sarah. "It's hopeless," she said after reading about the uncomplicated way to solve family problems. "I've tried all the things the book talks about and none of it works in my family. I feel like a total failure as a wife and mother. I've tried expressing my feelings openly and honestly to my husband and children, but they just don't respond. Dan either gets mad or he completely clams up. And the kids act like my feelings are a total embarrassment to them. I suppose that's natural for teenagers, but it really hurts me. I've tried having a regular time for discussing family issues, but it doesn't work. My son takes his cue from his father — they both just sit there looking sullen. And what's my daughter's reaction? 'Mom, you're weird.'"

Hitting the Wall

Sarah's dilemma may have a familiar ring to other recovering people. Here we are, making sincere efforts to do all the good things that are supposed to improve marriage and family life and promote our personal growth, and what happens? We run into a brick wall.

What good did roundtable discussions do Sarah when her daughter wouldn't take off the stereo headphones and her husband and son refused to talk? A sample family discussion:

"Gimme a break, Mom, don't be weird."
"What's there to talk about? I don't get it."
"It's not my problem. Drop it."

What good were regular family outings when the kids griped the whole time that they'd rather be with their friends and their father threatened to slap their ugly mouths if they didn't shut up? And how could Sarah ask Grandma and Grandpa to take the kids for the weekend when Grandpa drank a fifth of vodka every day?

The techniques counselors and authors suggest for improving marriage and family life sound intelligent and practical on paper. Yet the techniques don't often work in real life. Establishing good communication with the people we love is far more complicated than merely expressing our feelings. Let's look at three common complications:

1. What happens to communication when we express ourselves clearly, nondefensively, and honestly, but our partner isn't the least bit interested in listening?
2. What happens when our partner listens openly and lovingly, but our expressions of feeling are actually unreasonable demands distorted by anger, bitterness, and past hurts?
3. What happens when we walk around feeling like a time bomb about to explode, but the rest of the family members want to keep the status quo?

Many of the psychologists, counselors, and authors who advocate "Improved Communication" as the path to a good relationship seem to live in an unreal world, a utopian society, where everyone is cooperative, fair, and reasonable. *They assume that people who live together and love each other want nothing more than to make their partner feel happy and loved.*

Wrong!

Human beings are far more complex than that. Strong emotions such as anger, fear, guilt, shame, envy, and jealousy color our perceptions and motivate our behavior. This is true for everyone, but for those of us who have had to deal with chemical dependency problems, these normal emotions become intensified.

Even in recovery, resentments over past hurts can make us act like fools, or witches, or brutes, or devils. And unless we've made a real effort to know ourselves better, we often won't understand why we act that way or why our love relationships so often leave us feeling frightened, alone, and betrayed.

Pat Answers and Obvious Solutions

When our love life is a mess, we often have difficulty solving our problems because we react emotionally rather than logically. Strong emotions block our ability to think straight. We crave obvious, simple solutions for confusing, complex problems. Thus we are drawn to pat answers, ready-made and off-the-rack pop psychology.

Pat answers sound *so right*, so apt and fitting. That's the allure. But in life outside the storybooks, major problems don't get resolved permanently, now and forever in three easy steps.

Ann, a thirty-year-old grocery checker, recalls a six-month period when she and her husband, Paul, were on the verge of a split. "I don't believe I could think at all when our marriage was falling apart. I went from anger to depression. I felt let down, bitterly disappointed. I was outwardly calm and poised most of the time, but I was crumbling inwardly. Think rationally? I couldn't concentrate on anything long enough to think at all. What I wanted most was a very simple, tidy, and painless solution. So at a friend's suggestion, I took a course in communication skills. I had this wild hope that if I could just learn to communicate better, our marriage would be saved. During class, I role-played some of the situations in my marriage with other class members. It worked like a charm! But when I got home, everything was different. My husband wouldn't cooperate. I got flustered and forgot what I was supposed to say. We ended up screaming at each other."

The Hard Solution: Facing Internal Chaos

Selma's father was an alcoholic and she married a man who drank heavily and dabbled with other drugs. She summed up her experience in her youth and married life this way: "I felt unloved and unappreciated. All the time. And I had this feeling inside me — *This Thing* — that scared me silly."

What was she frightened of? "Somehow I thought if I ever let *This Thing* out, my entire world would explode." To prevent this destructive force from ruining her life, she buried a lot of her bad feelings and resentments — a common reaction to chemical dependency in families.

Unfortunately, soft and tender feelings get buried too. After having our vulnerabilities stomped on a time or two, displays of affection and words of love can seem too dangerous to risk. In the end, we may become so out of touch with our emotions that all we feel is confusion and a terrible, nameless anxiety.

Active chemical dependency and codependency make good communication impossible because we are in complete emotional and spiritual chaos. This chaos makes us generally incapable of feeling benevolent and warm toward others. We are in great pain. Although we may put on a loving facade (and we may think of ourselves as loving), our relationships with other people are essentially self-serving and filled with anger. Our main goal is to get other people to give us what we think we want and need. Despite our protests to the contrary, we care little about anyone but ourselves. We are guided by our own will. Indeed, *Alcoholics Anonymous* tells us we are victims of "self-will run riot." Our inner chaos generates defiance and dishonesty. When self-will runs riot, nothing and no one can ever please us for long.

Recovery forces us to confront our inner chaos and confusion, and when we do, it is one of the most shattering and painful experiences we can endure. It is also one of the most healing.

Superficial skill-building seems to promise a way to heal without the pain, without confronting our confusion. Skill-building then becomes an obstacle to recovery by allowing us to avoid the painful confrontation with self. What good are communications skills when our soul remains in chaos? How can we listen openly to other people when our self-will continues to scream, *My way is the only way!*

It's possible to enter a recovery program, to become abstinent, and to remain basically unchanged. One of the ways we remain unchanged is by seeking out easy and pat solutions to the critical problem of the chaos in our being. Superficial skill-building is one of those pat answers that leads nowhere. We must be willing to look honestly and deeply into our chaotic thoughts and emotions. We must patiently and persistently assess and reassess our lives. We must have the courage to face the unacceptable, the frightening, the painful.

Too Good to be True

Many codependents hide from their internal chaos by putting on a happy face during family sessions when their loved one is in a treatment program. They are long on communication skills and short on integrity.

Take Susan, for example. She always came in smiling, usually with a tray of home-baked cookies. She always had a kind word, a gentle touch, an understanding nod for other group members and the treatment staff. "I'm just very grateful for this program," she said every week. Yes, she had suffered a lot, she admitted, and when other group members talked of their pain, Susan would nod wisely, then offer an apt quote from the treatment literature she had taken home and memorized.

Susan always knew the right thing to say. She listened attentively, she shared portions of her own story. Yet, every moment she was censoring herself, making sure she only revealed those things that made her look good, made her look like a hero.

She'd been in individual therapy before and had read a number of self-help books, so she knew it was important for her to "own" her feelings. She certainly didn't want to look like she was in denial. Susan had become therapy-wise. She had learned to hide behind her excellent communication skills and her knowledge of therapy techniques.

People like Susan fear that if they step off their pedestal of goodness and understanding they will be labeled *bad people* or *failures* and they will somehow be blamed for all the family problems. They present themselves as concerned, caring, perhaps deeply hurt, but ready to help and forgive and understand. "All I want," they say, "is for my loved one to get better."

While they may shine like beacons of understanding and acceptance, and they may be truly helpful to other group members, they are actually behaving in a fashion that is self-destructive and destructive to their loved ones.

It's normal to have bad feelings when you or someone you love is messed up with chemical dependency and all the problems that come with it. It is completely abnormal to be constantly helpful and understanding, no matter what the situation. This false cheerfulness springs from denial and the fear of looking bad to other people. While wanting to look like a good person is a natural reaction, it can prevent us from facing painful truths which must be dealt with if healing is to occur. We all make mistakes, we all have done things in our families that may have been less than wonderful, we may even have been selfish and cruel.

When we present ourselves as always good and right and just, we are being fraudulent. Group members who present themselves as untarnished examples of good will, innocence, and understanding are usually the most troubled and resistant to change. They will leave the group unchanged, their halos shining, and they will go home to create havoc and destruction.

The most basic requirement of intimacy is honesty. We must take off our halos and become honest with ourselves, admitting our defects and inner chaos. As *Alcoholics Anonymous* states: "If you have already made a decision, and an inventory of your grosser handicaps, you have made a good beginning. That being so you have swallowed and digested some big chunks of truth about yourself."

Myth: Just Learn to Express Yourself

One of the big chunks of truth we need to digest is that during the first stages of recovery we're going to have a lot of bad, ugly, horrid, poisonous feelings. And while these feelings are real, they're not always *valid*.

What's the difference between a real feeling and a valid one? Any emotion a person experiences is "real." For example, if a woman looks out the window and sees her husband in a passionate embrace with another woman, the surge of emotion she feels is real. If the man isn't really her husband, but only a guy that looks like him from behind, and she continues to be furious with her husband, then her real emotions are not valid.

In chemical dependency, we suffer from a lot of real emotions that are based on invalid assumptions, beliefs, and perceptions. Drinking and other drug use distort our feelings so much that in the beginning of recovery it's difficult to know what's valid and what isn't.

Expressing our real feelings, if those feelings are invalid, can be dangerous. Unless we have sincerely examined the riotous nature of our self-will and started on the process of making amends and corrections, expressing ourselves to others can actually be an obstacle to resolving intimacy issues.

Strange as it may seem, self-expression can be a barrier to communication. "Listen," says Wanda, "I know all the books say it's crucial to be open and honest about your feelings, but God! — all the time?" Her husband, Ken, had gone through treatment for chemical dependency and was in an aftercare group, a tough-minded, no-nonsense group that has the motto, "When the going gets tough, the tough get going."

Wanda felt that communication with Ken was even harder than it had been before treatment. "I mean, his favorite word is 'bullshit.' If he doesn't agree with me, I'm full of bullshit. If he thinks I'm not expressing my true feelings 100 percent of the time, it's bullshit. It's almost like he's got this reflex, so if he hears something that makes his brain twitch or something, out comes 'bullshit.' God, it gets so boring."

But that's not the worst of it, Wanda says. "He gets on this bullshit high-horse around my friends, and they don't understand any of it. And most of the time it isn't even honest. He thinks he's being honest and insightful, but I really think he's being an emotional bully."

The Hazards of Emotional Dumping

In his book, *Feelings*, psychiatrist Willard Gaylin argues against the "emotions as pus" concept, which goes like this: "Emotions must be discharged into the environment. . . .You must bring your anger to a head — and if you cannot, the good doctor will lance the boil and discharge the venom. What must be expressed is almost always anger — occasionally anxiety."

The emotions as pus principle, says Gaylin, has found favor in our culture among a diverse group who have glorified self-expression, using the credo, "Let it all hang out."

Gaylin argues, "I have never felt that people's inner feelings have some claim to public recognition. Quite the contrary: for the most part, the private life of the narcissist, like the private parts of the exhibitionist, ought not be hung out — uninvited — in the public space."

Unless we have confronted and made peace with our inner chaos, much of our unexpressed emotion will be self-serving, narcissistic, infantile, and mean. Spewing all of this junk out on our loved ones serves no positive purpose. It does not create intimacy, it destroys it.

But get the junk out we must. And that's exactly what counselors, ministers, and psychiatrists are for. These professionals can help us sort through our pain, our anger, and our fears.

The Fifth Step of Alcoholics Anonymous counsels us to admit "to God, to ourselves, and to another human being the exact nature of our wrongs." As we're rummaging around inside our souls taking our inventory, we're going to be stirring up lots of violent and painful feelings. These feelings are raw, unprocessed, and frequently ugly. If we subscribe to the let-it-all-hang-out theory of communication, we may think we're honestly living up to the Fifth Step when we dump all our emotional garbage on our loved ones.

Wrong!

Dumping unprocessed emotional sewage on a friend or mate is not an act of love. It's relationship pollution of the worst kind. *Alcoholics Anonymous* tells us: ". . . we cannot disclose anything to our [spouses] or our parents which will hurt them and make them unhappy. We have no right to save our own skin at another person's expense. Such parts of our story we tell to someone who will understand, yet be unaffected. The rule is we must be hard on ourself, but always considerate of others."

If we are wise, we will search out a detached and objective professional, someone who can help us sort through all of our internal junk without personal prejudice. We need someone who won't be hurt by our pain, who won't feel attacked by our anger, who won't be scared away by our fear.

It's too much to expect a friend or spouse to fill that role for us, especially during the early stages of recovery when we're still wild-eyed and totally mixed up. Remember: The people closest to us are mixed up too. They're as hurting and confused as we are, even if they don't look like it.

The person we choose to unload on must understand chemical dependency, and must be mentally and emotionally prepared to listen to us without judging us harshly. And they must know how to keep our story confidential.

Few spouses or lovers fit this description. They are too emotionally enmeshed in our lives to be able to hear the voice of our confusion and pain above their own shrieking loneliness and despair. If we are truly attempting to be less selfish toward others, we must also be willing to respect the pain our partner may be feeling.

Somewhere along the line, we're going to have to learn how to share our innermost thoughts and feelings with the people we love. But we don't need to do this on Day One of recovery. It may take weeks or months before we can honestly express ourselves without causing a major emotional sewage spill. We must be patient. We can't and won't become intimacy experts overnight. But slowly, as we work daily on our program of recovery, we are becoming the kind of person who can feel and express positive feelings, like love, joy, and serenity.

Listening: The Other 50 Percent

At this point, we may find ourselves in a double-bind. It's dangerous for us to keep all of our feelings bottled up inside and it's dangerous for us to let them out. What do we do? This is the place where involvement in a recovery group, in group therapy, or in a support group can be a lifesaver.

Much of popular psychology urges us to unload, to get what we're feeling and thinking off our chests. Recovering people who are in the process of getting in touch with their sober feelings might try a different tactic: *Shut up and listen.*

One thing most alcoholics, other addicts, and codependents have in common is a feeling of isolation. We tend to believe our feelings are unique, that no one could ever understand or help us. This belief is a form of grandiosity. The truth is that human beings are capable of a wide range of emotions — all people, all emotions, all flavors, colors, and intensities. What we are feeling others have felt. This is true for even our most terrible, agonizing secrets.

One of the reasons we feel so alone, isolated, and weird is because we tend to place too much emphasis on our own thoughts, needs, and feelings. This makes us self-centered and insensitive. In other words, we think no one could understand or feel the way we do because we've never bothered to ask questions or listen or pay attention to anyone or anything but ourselves. On the flip side, some of us have been so preoccupied with what other people want and feel that we've become numbed to our own feelings. We think our feelings don't matter, so we ignore them.

If we feel totally out of sync with other people, we can develop a terrible fear of self-expression. We may think our needs and feelings are so weird and unacceptable that we have no right to express them. Or we may fear that if we do express ourselves, something terrible will happen.

By attending recovery meetings with an open mind and a closed mouth, we may begin to see our feelings aren't so weird after all. We may even discover there are hundreds of other people who have felt the kind of rage, fear, and despair we have known. Not only have they experienced it, they have triumphed over it. If we truly listen we may begin to learn how other people have reached the healthy balance point between stuffing down emotions and loosing an emotional fire storm on innocent bystanders.

Remember: At least 50 percent of communication — perhaps the most important half — is *listening*.

Weird Like the Rest of Us

A note: We don't have to sit totally mute. The goal is to listen to other people without judging them harshly and to apply what we learn from them to our own lives. Sometimes we can speed our learning by *asking questions*.

For example, Bill was having a terrible time getting over his ex-wife, a woman who scoffed at his sobriety and who continued to use drugs. She had left him several months earlier and had filed for divorce. There was little hope of reconciliation. Bill still loved her, still ached for her in the middle of the night, still thought about her and the life they might have had together.

"You've got to get on with your life, Bill," his recovery group members advised.

"She's poison for your sobriety. You've got to get over her."
"Forget her."

"It's normal to grieve a lost love, Bill, but for your own good, get her out of your system. If you don't get her out of your mind, you're risking your sobriety."

Intellectually, Bill knew his friends were right. But emotionally, he still felt a terrific sense of loss. He started thinking there was something wrong. *I shouldn't be feeling this way, so sad, so empty. I shouldn't still be thinking about her.* He looked at other people who had gone through with divorce and they had started over. *Why can't I? Am I some sort of emotional weakling? Or what?*

One day he asked a counselor who had gone through a similar devastating break up and bounced back how long it usually took for someone to get over a broken heart.

"Oh, let's see," the counselor said. "It takes most people about two years, but it took me more like two and a half."

"Two years!" Bill was astounded. He and his wife had been separated for two months. "But the way everyone talked, I thought I should be completely over her by now. I felt like some sort of emotional wimp."

"Get serious, Bill. Look, you were married for twelve years, you loved her a lot. Believe me, you will get over her, but you'll never forget her. That's okay, give yourself some time. You're still in crisis right now. Get some counseling if you need it. But don't expect to forget her overnight. I think you're doing pretty good, considering you're still in the process of settling the divorce."

"You mean I'm not weird?"

The counselor laughed. "No, Bill, not weird."

It's common to continue having communication problems, even when we are well into recovery. If we have started taking our inventory, facing our chaos, and separating our valid emotions from our riotous self-will, we are then ready to begin sharing our thoughts and feelings with the people we love. It won't necessarily be easy. We might not get a hoped for response from the people we care about. And we may need the assistance of a counselor. This is all quite normal.

As we develop our ability to express ourselves, it's important that we remember the number one rule in intimacy: We are concerned about ourselves *and* others. Communication is about sharing. It's about talking *and* listening.

It may sound easy, but for people who are used to a life of selfishness or daily self-sacrifice, it's hard to learn how to both give and take. Hard, but worth it.

CHAPTER FIVE

Barrier #4: The Past

I tell you, the past is a bucket of ashes.
— *Carl Sandburg*

Recovery presents us with a great challenge. It requires us to move beyond anger, fear, and frustration. Recovery requires us to transcend the past — the oppressive obligations, hatreds, and injuries. In recovery we have the opportunity to change burning resentments and unyielding hostility into consideration, understanding, and acceptance of people who may have betrayed us before and who have the power to hurt us again. Unfortunately, many of us remain mortgaged to the past. Many of us find it easier to brood about past injustices, easier to fan the embers of old quarrels and humiliations, easier to keep old resentments alive, than to love, to accept, and to forgive.

Intimacy and Fear

Anxiety about emotional relationships often starts in childhood, centering on the most primal of human bonds — parent and child. During our formative years, many of us experienced the pain of feeling abandoned or rejected by people we loved. Perhaps one of our parents was cold, unloving, or bad-tempered. Or perhaps one of our parents was physically ill or emotionally unstable and unable to care for us adequately. Our parents may have had marriage problems and we interpreted their behavior as a rejection of ourselves. Or we may have suffered the loss of a parent through death or divorce.

Whatever the cause, many recovering people have internalized a deep fear of abandonment and rejection. This fear is neither rational nor reasonable. It's in the guts. Those of us who suffer from the fear of abandonment may appear full of confidence. We may seem to be self-assured, bold, daring, and resolute. Appearances deceive and mislead. All too often, beneath the thin veneer of pride and self-esteem, we feel unlovable and unworthy.

We seldom recall the exact events which first created our anxious feelings, but whenever we get in a similar situation we feel a flood of anxiety coming on. Unfortunately, the methods we choose to calm our distressing feelings often make our problems worse instead of better.

A deeply ingrained fear of abandonment makes it extremely difficult to enjoy a long-term intimate relationship because we have a tendency to view our partner's actions through the dark lens of our own anxiety. It's hard for us to accept love when we believe we are basically unlovable. It's difficult to give love when we anticipate the pain of another rejection.

Now listen, because this is important: If we suffer from the fear of abandonment and rejection, a lover can do many things to make us feel unloved and alone. *But there is little our lover can do to make us feel lovable and secure.* If we don't believe we are worthy of another person's affection, we will distrust love, we will distrust ourselves, and we will distrust the people who say they care about us.

Rotten and Unloved

Greg is a prime example of someone who believes at the center of his soul that he is flawed and unlovable. On the surface, he appears to be a man who has it all together. At age thirty-nine, he's been sober for six years and he's still active in a recovery program. He makes his living as a professional mental health counselor, and he's good at his job.

He's a keen listener, a perceptive interpreter of body language, and he's tactfully assertive when it's time to express his feelings and thoughts. Unlike many men, he's willing to talk openly about his feelings. His female co-workers pay him the high compliment of calling him a "sensitive guy." But his ex-wife and former lovers might disagree with that description.

Greg says, "I can't seem to keep a relationship going for more than a year or two. At first, when every day is exciting, it's easy for me to ignore irritating or inconsiderate things my girlfriend does. But after awhile, my resentments start building up. Little things bug me. When that happens it's just a matter of time before we break up."

Greg is truly baffled by his inability to make a lasting emotional connection with a woman. He's smart enough to see a repeating pattern in his behavior, but he's unable to change it. "I really loved my last girlfriend," he explains. "She was a good woman and I wanted that relationship to work. I couldn't wait to be with her, but whenever we got together, something happened. Little things she did and said bugged me. I'd start picking away at her, criticizing her, challenging her, until she'd lash back at me. We'd both say ugly things to each other, things I suppose we didn't really mean, but they hurt just the same. We'd both go away feeling rotten and unloved. In time, there was nothing more for us to say to each other. We broke up. And, except for the details, that's exactly the same way my ex-wife and I ended it."

Perhaps you, too, know what it's like to feel rotten and unloved. Some of us, like Greg, flee whenever these bad feelings invade a love affair. Other people hang on for dear life, practically twisting themselves inside out trying to please the critical partner. Still others cope by turning off their emotions, becoming numb and unresponsive to their partner.

These relationships *hurt.* Yet, despite all the pain, most of us are not willing to give up on the idea of love. Oh, we may pull back for a while, we may withdraw to nurse our wounds, but a part of us still longs for the warmth and security of the old-fashioned man and woman 'til death do us part kind of love affair.

That kind of love requires us to invest ourselves in a relationship over a long period of time with no guarantee of future profit. It demands that we open up, trust, and share our lives with a person who might disappoint or betray us. It requires us to relate to another human being who may have desires, beliefs, and goals different from our own.

When we risk intimacy, we have no way of knowing if love will enrich us or destroy us. Unfortunately, many of the survivors of chemical dependency know only too well that love hurts.

Greg's Turbulent Past

Greg knew how to express his feelings, needs, and desires, and he knew how to listen. But he was unwilling to make the investment or take the risks that true intimacy requires. He kept women at arm's length, substituting superficial verbal skills for emotional awareness. Evasive and unaware, he couldn't understand why he felt so empty and alone even when he was in love.

Perhaps it's no coincidence that Greg suffered a great deal of rejection as a child. Both of his parents loved him, but their own lives were so full of conflict and turbulence they were unable to offer him a sense of emotional security. His father drank too much and his mother had periodic bouts of severe depression. When his parents were in one of their "bad moods," they criticized Greg savagely, insulting him, putting him down, and accusing him of being a selfish and ungrateful brat.

A few hours later the mood would change and his mother would cling to him with a maudlin show of affection and maternal love. "You are my life," his mother told him. "Without you, I couldn't live." Then, in awhile, the insults and accusations started again.

That's what made the situation so crazy. When Greg came

home from school he never knew if he would be yelled at or hugged. Neither of his parents ever came straight out and rejected him. Greg thought he could've coped with that because at least he would've known exactly where he stood. Instead, his parents gave him love with one hand and ripped it away with the other. As a consequence, young Greg came to associate love and affection with hurt and rejection.

Greg's experience is not unusual. It would certainly be wonderful if all children grew up in stable homes with loving parents who consistently met the emotional needs of their children. Common sense tells us that reality is far different from that ideal scene. After all, parents are human too. They make mistakes. They have fears and doubts. They undergo emotional crises. And, unfortunately, parental mistakes can have a deep impact on a child's thoughts and emotions. In fact, our childhood hurts can help shape our beliefs about how intimate relationships operate.

Greg studied psychology in college because he wanted to understand how the human mind and emotions responded to childhood trauma. He became an expert on defense mechanisms and personality disorders. But because he'd never consciously confronted his own belief that everyone who loved him would also reject him, his childhood pain followed him into adult relationships. The hurt child inside him "knew" that every woman who loved him would eventually find him lacking in some way. Wasn't that the way it had always been? Anticipating the feared rejection created more anxiety than he could bear.

In short, intimacy scared Greg silly. His experiences as a child had convinced him that women were unpredictable and untrustworthy. What he waited for with every woman he loved was the moment when she would turn on him.

So instead of waiting for that dreaded moment, he attacked first. He expressed his feelings by finding fault, criticizing, sulking, and rejecting. It was easier that way. It saved his feelings and his face. It made him feel like a man inside, a man in control of his life, not some scared kid waiting for the axe to fall.

Pause for a moment now and consider these questions:

- Is it possible that you are allowing childhood hurts to govern your adult relationships?
- Are you feeling like a scared kid waiting for the axe to fall?
- Are you suffering from the belief that because you were hurt and rejected as a child you will inevitably be hurt and rejected by everyone you love?

Listen: At every stage of life we must make decisions about what is important and what is not. We must change and grow and reassess our beliefs about ourselves and the world around us. The judgments we made in childhood must be examined in light of broader adult knowledge. If we refuse to consciously update the mistaken or distorted beliefs we formed as children, we become slaves to the past — scared kids unable to enjoy the freedoms and privileges of adulthood.

A person who has been hurt by love, either as a child or adult, may develop a strong desire to avoid the anxiety intimacy creates. But shrinking from intimacy renders our relationships empty and meaningless, and cuts us off from the deepest pleasures life offers.

Greg had been fully active in a recovery program for years, and he had gone through the motions of self-confrontation. Yet he had refused to take his own searching moral inventory and make the necessary corrections and amends. Because of his failure to look deeply into his soul, his intimate life was a wreck. Physically, he was a grown man. But emotionally, he was still that scared and unloved child of the past.

Love Heals

We've all heard the wise sayings about the importance of loving ourselves and forgiving the people who have hurt us. But the wise sayings are often hellishly frustrating because they don't come with a map or a blueprint on how to accomplish love and forgiveness when we're filled with resentment and painful memories. When we've been terribly wounded by life — disappointed time and again — it's hard to go on believing in the ancient wisdom that says the path to inner peace opens to us when we decide to give selfless love to others, a love that demands no return on the investment.

In *Love, Medicine & Miracles*, Dr. Bernie Siegel, a surgeon who works with cancer patients, writes about the patient who has difficulty giving and receiving love:

> Many people . . . grow up believing there is some terrible flaw at the center of their being, a defect they must hide if they are to have any chance for love. Feeling unlovable and condemned to loneliness if their true selves become known, such individuals set up defenses against sharing their innermost feelings with anyone. They feel their ability to love shriveling up, which leads to further despair. Dostoyevsky expressed the feeling when he wrote, "I am convinced the only Hell which exists is the inability to love." Because such people feel a profound emptiness inside, they come to see all relationships and transactions in terms of *getting* something to fill the vaguely understood void within. They give love only on condition that they get something for it, whether comfort, security, praise, or a similar love. This "if" love is exhausting and prevents you from expressing your authentic self. It leads to an even deeper sense of emptiness, which keeps the vicious circle going.

While Dr. Seigel aimed his observations primarily at cancer patients, his words apply with equal force to folks whose lives have been conflicted by chemical dependency.

Many recovering people have a hard time accepting two life-transforming truths:

1. *You are no longer that frightened, powerless, rejected child of your*

past. You don't have to spend the rest of your life doing the same destructive things over and over again. You are not a needle stuck on a broken record, doomed to repeat a single line forever — *love, anxiety, rejection . . . love, anxiety, rejection . . .*
2. *Love heals.* A loving, caring relationship can help heal the past. Not just being loved — but being able to love, being able to care unselfishly, to be considerate and kind. You may instinctively know that a relationship with someone who truly loves you would be the answer to your problems. And you are right. All you need is one person you can really count on and trust, one person to nurture and love you, someone who will be both gentle and firm, and always caring. And that person is you.

You must develop the capacity to love and to care for yourself before you can develop a loving relationship with another. Only when you have learned to love and accept yourself, will you have it in you to love and accept another unselfishly.

So, yes, love does heal. And the most healing power of love comes from the love that radiates from within.

Getting Help

No question about it, developing a love relationship with another person can be hard. Love requires more than feelings of attraction and desire for the other person. Love requires a thoughtful and sometimes painful confrontation with your self.

Look at your life. As senseless and chaotic as it may seem, there is probably a pattern you can pick out. You may feel alone and unloved, yet you are part of an interdependent scheme with numerous others — a part of all humankind. Every action has a reaction. Every cause has an effect. Even when you feel totally powerless and victimized, you are both *action* and reaction, both *cause* and effect. You have great power to create happiness, yet, like Greg, you have probably spent much of your life creating unnecessary pain for yourself and others.

In everything there is a pattern, and in the patterns of your life lie the answers to much of your troubles and loneliness. By looking for the patterns you can begin to make sense out of what may seem like unending and senseless personal pain. Your job now, as an adult in the process of recovery, is to examine the beliefs, thoughts, and actions that form the patterns of your life.

Finding the patterns is hard, and knowing what do with this information once we find it is harder still. Some people can detect the important patterns in their lives and with patience and persistence can sort the conflicts out on their own. But others may need professional help.

How do we know when we need the assistance of a therapist? When our lives are stuck like a needle in a broken record. . . . When we keep doing the same dumb things over and over again. . . . When — try as we might — we can't seem to change our painful behavior for more than a few days or months at a time. . . . That's when we need a professional therapist to help us overcome the barrier caused by the pain of our past.

You may have been hurt in the past, but that doesn't mean you have to go through the rest of your life wounded and broken. You are not damaged goods. You are a complex person, perhaps a little mixed up, yet capable of deep insight and change. Capable, too, of loving and being loved.

CHAPTER SIX

Barrier #5: Role Strain

In 1952, *Life* magazine published an article on "The Wife Problem." This article informed the nation that research clearly showed that a man's upward climb in the business world depended greatly upon what kind of wife he had. The "good wife is good by *not* doing things — by *not* complaining when her husband works late; by *not* fussing when a transfer is coming up; by *not* engaging in any controversial activity."

In short, one of the most widely circulated and highly respected magazines in the United States told men and women that a desirable wife was passive, noncomplaining, inconspicuous, and forever adapting to the needs of her husband.

In 1952, when *Life* spoke, people listened.

Life and the Legacy of Rectitude

Now, you might wonder what a moldy article in a forty-year-old magazine has to do with love relationships in the present. After all, times have changed. Women make up 51 percent of the work force. Only a small minority of arch-conservatives still publicly advocate that a woman's proper role in life is to be her husband's uncomplaining servant.

Yet, the 1950s concept of the good wife and good husband rubbed off on all of us, if not directly, then (for those of us over thirty) through the influence of our parents. The affluence and placidity of the 1950s were like a safe harbor to our people who lived through the turbulence of World War II and the Great Depression. More than anything, they wanted safety, security, and a little bit of the good life. If it took a conformist mentality to attain those things, so be it. After what they'd been through, who can blame them for embracing a rigid viewpoint?

So many of our parents, and those of us who are over thirty years old, formed some of our most important beliefs about life at a time when male and female roles were as rigid as hard plastic:

- Men provided; women nurtured.
- Men made the living; women made the home life.
- A good husband made the decisions; a good wife supported those decisions.

A man could consider himself a man if he had a job that allowed him to provide his family with a home and food, health care and education, attractive clothes and recreation. For him, a good job was the essence of a good life. The money, status, and prestige that came from his work allowed him to also enjoy marriage, family, and home.

After the uncertainty and hardship of the Great Depression and the war years, women dug in on the home front with a vengeance. Television programs reflected and reinforced the social changes. TV moms Harriet Nelson (Mother in "Ozzie and Harriet") and June Cleaver (Mother in "Leave It To Beaver") became role models of the ideal wife and mother. For the wife in this role model, marriage, family, and home became the essence of a good life. A successful husband was the element which allowed her to enjoy money, status, and prestige.

The 1950s and early 1960s were a crucial time in American history, one that determined many of the values we live with today. Some of those values may now seem distant, quaint, or even ridiculous. Yet we cannot deny the importance this period in history still has on our lives.

But times change. On November 22, 1963, President Kennedy was assassinated — the first in a series of assassinations — and we, as a nation, lost our innocence. In 1964, President Johnson breathed life into John Kennedy's almost dead Civil

Rights Act and pushed it through Congress. Although this piece of legislation seemed primarily aimed at giving voting rights to Southern blacks, it had far-reaching consequences for all of us. Many people started saying women ought to have equal rights too.

In the late 1960s, the last vestiges of the gray-flannel conformity of the 1950s unraveled. A whole generation of young people thumbed their noses at the values of their elders. It was a time of movements — anti-war, free speech, women's liberation, open marriage, black power, drugs, sex, and rock and roll. We haven't been the same since. And many of us are glad for the changes.

Values in Conflict

But stop and think for a moment: How much have we really changed? Look deep into your own heart. What is it you really value? Despite the drastic changes in lifestyle and culture, two things have remained constant from the 1950s to now.

1. *For most women, a loving relationship with a man, a happy family, and a comfortable home remain the most essential ingredients of a good life.* Her career, her own personal life, and her individual development may be important, but those things are secondary on her list of priorities.
2. *For most men, challenging and rewarding work is still the most essential ingredient in a good life.* A loving relationship, a family, and home may be important, but most of his energies are channeled toward work and his own personal life.

Many couples today find themselves split right down the middle, straddling two sets of conflicting values. They have one foot in the Have-It-All present where women are supposed to have careers and men are supposed to be sensitive and vulnerable, and the other foot in the Conventional 1950s where women are supposed to take care of the home and children, and men are supposed to be strong, unruffled providers.

The traditional roles — man the provider, woman the nurturer — no longer apply for most couples. Many men *want* to be emotionally involved with their families. And most women work because the family *needs* the income her job provides. Marriage, family, and intimate relationships operate under a new and different set of rules to meet with a new, and sometimes disturbing, set of social and economic realities. Consider the impact of these few stark facts:

- Roughly half of all marriages will end in divorce.
- Few divorced women will receive alimony.
- Half of court-awarded child support will never be paid.
- Half the mothers of young children will work outside the home.
- There is a nationwide shortage of affordable child care centers.

Life today is far different than it was during the 1950s. But deep within our psyches, many of us hold a vivid picture of that earlier, seemingly more orderly time.

Flashback. It's three o'clock in the afternoon. Harriet and June are in their respective kitchens dishing out the chocolate chip cookies and cold milk for Rickie and The Beaver who are just home from school. Ozzie and Ward are still at the office, the house is spotless, and June's immaculate pearls glimmer in the warm kitchen light.

Ah, yes. It was a simpler time and place. Orderly. Pleasant. And even if the television shows didn't mirror life as people really lived it, they did represent a national ideal. Even those of us who hold "sitcom reality" in contempt may find — to our surprise — that we secretly cling to a childhood longing for the kind of family life enjoyed by Rickie and The Beaver.

Chemical Dependency and Roles under Stress

Traditional roles are shifting as a result of the complex forces of social and cultural change. This shift occurs in all countries, accelerating with the pace of technological advancement. While these shifts in values and traditional roles may cause confusion, the changes are not necessarily bad. The breakdown of rigid gender roles allows men to experience more emotional freedom and sensitivity. Women gain personal power, competence, and independence. These positive changes can help us broaden our perspectives and become more capable and competent.

But chemical dependency causes a negative and often irreversible erosion in roles, an erosion that shrinks our potential for growth, rather than expanding it. When Mom becomes dependent on alcohol or other drugs, she can no longer be relied on to fix meals. She abandons housekeeping and shopping. She becomes emotionally distant and unpredictable. Dad and the kids take up the slack. Mom is no longer consulted on major decisions affecting the family. The oldest daughter becomes, in effect, a substitute mother who does the housework and provides the nurturance and support.

At first, some observers might see Mom's neglect of household responsibilities as a positive thing. Why, they ask, should a woman be a slave to her family? Dad and the kids *should* take up the slack.

The problem is that Mom's addiction doesn't create a *sharing* of responsibility. The chemically dependent woman does not abandon boring household chores so she can devote her energies to other worthy pursuits. Instead, she abdicates her role as a fully active, contributing member of the family.

The same goes for the chemically dependent man who can no longer be counted on to assure a roof over the heads of his family and food on the table. He's not asking his family to *share* in the burden of creating a home. He's not democratically discussing the issue of family responsibilities. He's *demanding* that they take care of themselves while he squanders family resources on the whims, desires, and obsessions of his addiction.

When a man or woman stops functioning in their normal family roles, other family members assume the major roles by default. While it's good for a man to know how to cook and clean and for a woman to know how to pay bills and do household repairs, the manner in which these responsibilities are shifted in a chemically dependent family is always categorically unhealthy.

If Dad becomes financially undependable, Mom and the kids must take over his traditional role if the family is to survive. They become the providers and protectors.

In most chemically dependent families, the man continues to work and bring home a paycheck, but his work may be spotty and he may squander large amounts of money on himself. So even though the annual tax return may show a respectable income, the family may be suffering severe financial insecurity.

In a situation like this, the takeover of the husband's role of provider and protector may be covert, hidden, unacknowledged. The oldest son may start feeling it's his job to protect Mom and the younger children. The family may even find they can do without Dad. They can survive, and Dad is no longer necessary as a husband or a father. No longer essential, he becomes like a distant relative — an often unwanted relative, an embarrassment who simply makes life more difficult. Father no longer knows best.

Repeat: When one of the partners becomes addicted to alcohol or other drugs, it's not a question of the couple deciding to shift roles and share responsibilities. Instead, the addicted partner abandons customary duties, and the other partner takes over in order to keep disaster at bay. This takeover by default is usually reluctant and involuntary, accompanied by deep resentments, feelings of betrayal, and contempt for the partner's failures.

Eddie and Gerda

The conflict between Eddie and Gerda can help us understand how shifting roles can become a barrier to intimacy, especially after recovery begins. Many of us expect that recovery will automatically cause our relationships and family life to settle down into a more stable, normal, and happy routine. That's not necessarily true in the first days of recovery. Now, don't let that discourage you. If both partners are willing to change, compromise, and grow, stability and happiness will eventually be theirs. But in the first stages of recovery, we may have real difficulty adjusting to the new roles recovery creates for us.

Eddie, a newly sober alcoholic who works in construction, is learning about those adjustments. A family intervention session convinced him to seek treatment. His wife, Gerda, and his three children had all expressed deep love and concern for him, and had made him see how much his drinking was hurting all of them. They told him they needed him in the family, needed him strong and sober. Afraid of losing his job and deeply moved by their love, Eddie entered a chemical dependency treatment unit. After completing treatment, he expected a warm welcome home. Instead, he found himself frozen out of family life.

"I'm feeling pretty resentful right now," Eddie said after being home for a couple of months. "I thought my family would be glad I got sober, but they treat me like I'm some sort of outsider in my own home. Now that I can think straight, I want to know exactly how we stand financially. I make good money and so does my wife. I've started thinking about making some investments for our future security, but my wife won't talk. You know what I found? A bunch of bank statements hidden in the trunk of her car! She's got secret accounts she won't tell me about. When I asked her about them she told me to mind my own business. Do you believe that? As if the financial security of my family isn't my business."

In fact, for years Eddie had been a source of financial *inse*curity. Gerda says, "If I'd let Eddie handle our finances while he was drinking we would have ended up in the poor house. He spent money like water. A lot of impulse buying, trying to make himself look like a big man. Last year, he spent nine hundred dollars on a television set. Not for us. It was a wedding present for his niece. We couldn't afford that! My God, the color's so faded on our own TV — we might as well be watching black and white. But Eddie wanted to look like a big man in front of his brother. He didn't stop to think that we needed that money to pay our mortgage. Now, he's been sober for three months and all of a sudden he starts acting like he's some big financial expert. He tells me he's going to make investments for our future. Over my dead body! I'm not going to risk the small amount of security that I've created for myself and my kids so Eddie can feel like a big man."

In his drinking days, Eddie abdicated his role as a stable and reliable partner in family decisions. He acted on impulse. Many of his actions were irresponsible and selfish. Half the time, he had no idea how his family was operating on a day by day basis, partly because Gerda hid important information from him, but largely because he was too intoxicated or hungover to comprehend fully what was going on around him. Gerda became the rock of family stability.

With a few months sobriety under his belt, Eddie wanted to reclaim his lost role as head of the household. He wanted to regain the family's respect. And, he thought, the best way to do that was to take charge, make decisions, chart the course of the family's future.

Gerda resisted him every step of the way. The result: There was actually more conflict between them now, than when Eddie was still drinking.

Learning from Conflict

Almost all recovering couples will face similar conflicts. When one partner changes, it shifts responsibilities within the relationship, it upsets the status quo. As one partner grows stronger, the other may feel threatened and afraid.

Recovery does not automatically reinstate the old roles. In fact, other family members often resist attempts to reclaim the old role status. When Mom, fresh out of treatment, tries to resume her role, Dad and the kids think, *We got along fine without Mom when she was drunk all the time.* When Dad returns from treatment, Mom and the kids think, *Who needs him?*

The man who goes through treatment may find his wife has become much more independent, much more assertive than she used to be. She's had to assume additional family responsibilities and she may not be too eager to relinquish the power she has acquired. In the same vein, after going through treatment a woman may find family members grudging and even resentful when she attempts to resume her traditional role.

Eddie came home from treatment eager to reclaim his role as head of the household. But he failed to consider one important factor: Reclaiming his role meant dethroning Gerda. She'd been making the family decisions, holding everything together, and all of a sudden Eddie was trying to take that away from her. It wasn't until they agreed to see a marriage counselor together that they were able to resolve their differences.

The counselor helped them realize they were both making mistakes. Eddie approached his family with the finesse of a porcupine in a balloon factory. He decided on his own that he wanted to be head of the household again. He didn't consult Gerda, ask her opinion, or consider her feelings. He simply informed her that from now on he was going to handle the household finances. When she resisted, he felt attacked and betrayed.

After half a dozen counseling sessions Eddie admitted, "It was all ego on my part. I thought what I was doing was freaking magnificent. I fully expected Gerda and the kids to applaud my every move. For the life of me I couldn't figure out what Gerda's problem was. I was the man of the family again and I thought she should appreciate what I was doing. When she didn't go along with me, I accused her of being a castrating witch. Of course, that didn't help matters any."

Gerda had made some mistakes too. Over the years she had developed the habit of hiding important information from her husband. "It seemed," Gerda says, "that there was no problem that Eddie couldn't make worse. If I saved five dollars and Eddie found out about it, it was gone. If one of the kids had a small problem Eddie turned it into a catastrophe with his temper. I learned that the best way to keep the peace was to keep Eddie in the dark about what was really going on."

Gerda's biggest mistake was continuing this practice when Eddie got sober. With recovery, he was developing the capacity to be reliable and responsible, but Gerda continued to treat him as though he were a misbehaving adolescent. Even though she loved Eddie, her general attitude toward him was one of barely concealed contempt. As far as she was concerned, he'd been an inadequate husband in the past, and she'd be damned before she'd give him a chance to screw things up now.

Attitude Adjustment: Scrutinizing the Roles

Discovering the mistakes they were making was a beginning, but it wasn't enough to solve Eddie and Gerda's marital problems. Their counselor explained that all of us hold certain beliefs about ourselves and our partners. These beliefs motivate our behavior whether we consciously acknowledge them or not. When couples stop talking about their beliefs, as almost all chemically dependent couples do, the relationship becomes a breeding ground for conflict and resentment.

There's another element to complicate matters. Therapists who have studied the effect of chemical dependency on the family tell us that most family members lose sight of "normal" intimate behavior. Because life in an alcoholic home is filled with denial, pretense, and confusion, family members have to guess at how "normal" relationships work.

And usually we guess wrong. Eddie's estimate of normal male/female relationships came from James Bond novels and the *Penthouse* Forum. Gerda's idea of a normal husband was a man who was a cross between Tom Selleck and Ward Cleaver. Is it any wonder they were disappointed with each other?

Their counselor asked them to examine their underlying beliefs and assumptions by having each of them separately answer the following questions:

- What's your idea of a good husband?
- What's your idea of a good wife?
- Who should be responsible for family finances?
- Who should be responsible for housework? Yard work?
- Who should discipline the children?
- Who should be head of the household?
- Who should be in charge of major decisions? Minor decisions?
- Who should take the lead in sexual intercourse?
- Who should decide when and where to make love?
- Who should climax first?

There are no right or wrong answers to these questions. The questions are "loaded" on purpose, designed to tease out stereotyped, unrealistic, and unfair attitudes. These ten simple and apparently harmless questions force us to think about the unspoken — and often unthinkable — assumptions we make in everyday life about our roles and values. Once we get our thoughts and beliefs down on paper, we can then start talking about our role conflicts with our partner.

Eddie and Gerda discovered they were both clinging to rigid gender stereotypes that were creating a barrier in their relationship. Eddie's idea of a good husband was a man who was strong, silent, and decisive. If he was worried or doubtful, he'd spare his family anxiety by keeping his doubts to himself. And once he made a decision, he felt a good wife shouldn't try to weaken him by asking questions or complaining.

Gerda wanted to ask questions. She, too, thought a good husband was strong and decisive, but that silent business was for the birds. She wanted a man she could talk to. Yet, she admitted she had been just as silent and uncommunicative as her husband had been. She had somehow expected Eddie to "know" what she needed from him.

Like many other couples, they had never discussed their sexual likes and dislikes. They both considered sex to be "too personal" to talk about.

It took several months of weekly counseling sessions for Eddie and Gerda to hash out their differences. Eddie came to realize it was unreasonable for him to expect Gerda, who worked full time, to do all the housework and uncomplainingly submit to his authority.

Eddie also discovered something more disturbing: "I used to look at Gerda — and really *all* women — as sort of second-class citizens. I know it was unfair. I see that now, but it's still almost second nature."

He takes his insight a step further: "The hardest adjustment for me is to look upon Gerda as my equal, as a person in her own right. I know my old attitude must have done terrible things to her self-esteem, but I just didn't know any better. I grew up at a time when women were considered the weaker sex. My alcoholism kept me from growing with the times. Emotionally, I'm still somewhere back in 1962 — still going through the storm and stress of adolescence — but I'm catching up."

Gerda's catching up too. "I discovered that I'd been putting Eddie in a terrible bind. I wanted him to be 1950s strong, and I also wanted him to be sensitive and vulnerable. I just couldn't forgive him when he failed to meet my expectations."

Gerda's working on forgiving Eddie for his past mistakes and present weaknesses. She realized that when she married Eddie twenty-two years ago, she had expected him to never let her down, to solve her problems, and to make her happy. She had wanted him to share his emotions with her, but she refused to allow him to display any sign of weakness. She had reinforced his silence with her own unrealistic expectations of how a man should be. To break down the barrier of silence between them, she knew she had to accept her husband as a fallible, and sometimes weak and frightened human being.

Gerda and Eddie have come a long way toward healing the rift in their marriage. Eddie says, "By plowing through the garbage of our expectations and assumptions we were able to start looking at each other as real people instead of cardboard characters. I think we have more love and respect for each other now than any other time in our marriage."

Gerda has this advice for other recovering couples: "Eddie and I were too confused, too stubborn, and too resentful to solve our problems on our own. Marriage counseling made us look at ourselves and at each other with new eyes. I tell my friends who have a partner who refuses to get counseling to go on their own. I learned so much about myself! I had no problem seeing Eddie's defects, but when it came to myself, I was blind. I'm glad Eddie has changed, but to be honest, I'm most proud of my own changes. Here I am in my forties, and for the first time in my life, I'm truly happy."

CHAPTER SEVEN

Barrier #6: Damaged Trust

Trust is a complicated concept, and there are many interpretations about the nature of true trust.

"Trust me."

These two small words carry a lot of emotional freight. And with good reason. Civilization is built on trust. Human communities depend on trust. Trust is an essential factor in business and politics. And trust is vital in relationships.

"Trust me."

Politicians, advertisements, parents, lovers, and used car dealers — all in one way or another — say, "Trust me." And we do. We place our trust in parents, politicians, in consumer products, in lovers and friends and relatives — and, yes, we even place our trust in airline schedules and television evangelists.

Inevitably, we get burned. Our parents may let us down — by neglect, emotional or physical abuse, or by failing to nurture us during the critical years of early development when we are learning what to expect from people and from the world. Later in life, we are lied to by friends and lovers, teachers and politicians, advertisements, and salespersons.

If we get burned badly enough or often enough, we become distrustful. This is what happens most often in relationships marred by chemical dependency. Just as chemical dependency destroys intimacy, it also erodes trust.

The Seeds of Distrust

By the time he was forty-five, Harry had worked his way up to become manager of an auto parts store. But in the past three years, his drinking increased to the point that his family didn't know what to do. A pastor suggested family intervention. Harry's family, two good friends, and his boss cooperated. A skilled counselor guided the intervention, helping the participants prepare for a loving confrontation with Harry. The intervention covered many areas, but trust was at the core.

Harry's wife: "You're not your old self, not the Harry I married. The Harry I fell in love with would never have gotten drunk and passed out at Thanksgiving dinner. The Harry I fell in love with would never get drunk and make a pass at my best friend. I've heard your excuses and lies so often that I don't even listen anymore. I can't trust you. I don't even feel like I know you anymore."

Harry's son: "You used to be a lot of fun, even when you were working long hours. But now it's gotten so you don't care about us anymore. You keep saying you're going to come to one of our basketball games and watch me play, but something always comes up. Like last weekend. You missed the game again, came home drunk, and got in a big argument with Mom. You knocked over the lamp and then went to sleep on the couch. I know you were all apologetic the next day, but I've heard all your excuses and apologies before. I don't believe anything you say anymore."

Ralph, a friend: "Harry, we've talked about this before. I've told you you're getting into the bottle too much, and you always shine me on. My wife told me you've been making some suggestive comments when I'm not around. Before, I think we'd joke about something like this. But you've gotten real sneaky. And loud and obnoxious. I've come to the point where I don't even want to invite you over for Monday Night Football. You drink all of the booze and start an argument, and then blame me or Mike [another friend] for getting on your case."

Harry's boss: "Frankly, Harry, I haven't been able to depend on you for over a year. I've tried to make allowances because you've been with us for a long time, through some tough years. You've been a loyal, hard worker, and I admire that. But that hasn't been the case recently. I've listened to your excuses, and I've seen you try to shift responsibility when things screw up. Other people at the shop are tired of covering for you. You're not pulling your own weight. The bottom line is this: We need a whole man to manage the shop, someone we can rely on, not half a man who's only half there."

Harry's family, friends, and co-workers grew distrustful. They became wary. They learned not to expect too much. His friends became distant. His wife felt bitter and betrayed, and at the same time she feared abandonment. She couldn't count on Harry in a crisis. Harry *was* the crisis.

Trust Issues in Recovery

When chemical dependency erodes trust, distrust sets in. With a vengeance. When we get hurt in relationships, we set up barriers, defenses to protect us from getting hurt in the future. We may become distrustful, skeptical, and even cynical about recovery. Just like Humpty Dumpty, trust takes a great fall and shatters. And all the King's horses, and all the King's men can't put trust together again.

At least that was the way it seemed to Harry after treatment. Harry's wife was on edge, as if waiting — just waiting for him to slip and start drinking again. His friends told Harry they were happy he had the courage to get help, but they didn't seem too eager to get together. True, they did invite Harry over to watch Monday Night Football, but it turned out to be a tense and awkward evening, with uncomfortable silences during the beer commercials. Hardened by past disappointments, Harry's son no longer cared whether Harry came to a game or not. Harry's boss adopted a cautious "wait and see" attitude. Harry kept his job, but he was on probation. And everyone knew it.

This is the way Harry viewed it: "It's like I'm a mental case or something. Nobody trusts me at all. I get the feeling they're all just waiting to see me fall off the wagon, just waiting to see me start drinking and raising hell again. Not even that. It's like I'm constantly under surveillance. Are my eyes red in the morning from an allergy? Or was old Harry out on the town last night. Is that a new mouthwash I'm using? Or has old Harry got something to hide — or worse, has old Harry developed a taste for mouthwash?"

At times, he even felt like they were *hoping* he'd screw up again. "I'm like a season," he told his counselor during a session of aftercare. "Or a phase of the moon. Old Harry can be counted on to screw up every so often. There's spring, summer, fall, winter, and Harry-on-a-bender. It's like my drinking was so predictable, I'd become a strange sign of order in the universe, and they'll be disappointed if I stay sober."

Harry wasn't having paranoid fantasies. He wasn't the victim of an overactive imagination. Chemical dependency undermines the foundation of trust. Trust is built on honesty, consistency, and reliability, but chemical dependency fosters dishonesty, inconsistency, and unreliability. And in so doing, chemical dependency changes what others expect from us. Distrust usually builds up over a period of years, so it's only natural that distrust lingers after treatment.

Sobriety is necessary to restore trust, but sobriety alone will not eliminate distrust.

The Importance of Being Trustworthy

Books on intimacy usually encourage partners to become more trusting, to become more vulnerable, more open to risk. But we believe this advice is misguided in most instances, whether or not the relationship is conflicted by chemical dependency. We believe it's wrong to encourage partners to become more trusting without first establishing the ground rules for intimate trust. And the basic ground rule is: *First, become trustworthy.*

In a sense, trust is like credit. If you are reliable, pay your bills on time, have a good work history, and an income, you can usually get credit. On the other hand, if you're a deadbeat with a record of unpaid bills and a spotty work record, you'll probably have a hard time getting credit. But even if you have bad credit now, you can get credit in the future. You do that by taking care of old debts, having a regular income, money in the bank, and so on.

Some may find this comparison between credit and trust to be distasteful: "But you're comparing intimacy to business practices. A relationship isn't a business. Friends and family members aren't creditors constantly examining the books of our trust account."

Maybe not openly. But most of us learn from experience, and while we may not keep a running audit on each other's trustworthiness, we do learn over time who we can count on and who's more likely to let us down. Whether we know it or not, we do have a trust account. When we show that we are trustworthy, our trust account builds.

Some addicts and codependents have a magical expectation that chemical dependency treatment will automatically restore trust and intimacy, and they feel frustrated and let down when distrust lingers on.

Harry's wife struggled with her feelings: "Harry's sober now, and I feel like I should be able to trust him, but I just can't. It's really bad in bed. I still cringe whenever he touches me because I keep getting flashes of the times he came to bed drunk, smelling like stale cigarettes soaked in beer and sweat. Sometimes I think I've been conditioned like Pavlov's dog, only I didn't learn to salivate at the sound of a bell, I learned to shudder and feel nauseated at the smell of cigarettes soaked in beer and sweat. It's hard to rebuild trust, to rebuild a love life with those kinds of images floating around in my head."

Blind Trust Versus Diligent Distrust

There are tremendous social pressures to be more trusting, more open, more willing to risk. Risk what? In business deals, we risk money and reputation. In relationships, the risk is most often psychological — we face the chance of getting our feelings hurt, of being embarrassed, ridiculed, or betrayed.

Trust goes awry when we see only two alternatives — total blind trust and diligent distrust.

Blind trust consists of a kind of nonchalant gullibility, a sunny optimism, a tenacious, wistful belief that people will behave decently and will always do the right thing without having to be reminded. It's the optimism of Pollyanna, the "glad child" in Eleanor Porter's novel, *Pollyanna*, who always looked for the best in people.

It worked for Pollyanna, a fictional creation, but in the real world Pollyanna would be easily deceived. (Indeed, "polly-anna" has become a term of derision for someone who is gullible, foolishly and blindly trusting, and optimistic.) And so it is for those whose blind trust and optimism so often sadly, and even fatally, turns out to be misguided, misplaced.

The blindly trusting Pollyanna was a child, which makes sense because blind trust requires a childish belief in the power of wishful thinking. Young children believe their thoughts and actions control the world — that's one of the reasons children often feel unreasonable guilt when something bad happens to another person. Imagine two second graders in a playground dispute. Tiffany and Jason are fighting over possession of the Nerf ball. Jason wrests the ball from Tiffany's hands and runs away, calling her names and making faces as he skips along. Infuriated, seven-year-old Tiffany thinks, *I hate him! I wish a big rock would fall on him and squish him flat!* The next day, Jason is run over by a car.

Now, of course, Tiffany's wish had nothing to do with Jason's accident. But she doesn't know that. The typical seven-year-old mind doesn't understand coincidence, probability, and chance. Tiffany is stricken with guilt. She thinks if she hadn't wished for Jason to be squished, he wouldn't have been. In effect, she thinks her thoughts control the world.

So what does the magical thinking of children have to do with intimate relationships among adults? It's this: Many of us have never given up the magical belief that our thoughts can control the behavior of other people. We may even fear that merely raising questions in our minds about trust, about another person's deceit, is all it'll take to destroy a relationship. Better not think about it, then.

Alicia doesn't want to think about it. She's been noticing some disturbing signs in the behavior of her boyfriend, a man with a history of cocaine abuse. He'd emptied her bank account more than once to buy drugs. Then he straightened up . . . for a while. Now, he's staying out late, spending money and refusing to account for it. Early one morning she saw him pawing through her purse. Later she discovered forty dollars and her Visa card missing.

"I don't want to talk about these things — my questions, my reservations, my feelings of distrust," says Alicia. "If I do, he'll blame me, get angry, stomp off, and if he's not using now, my distrust could be enough to push him over the edge."

The magical thinking of blind trust goes like this: *I create my own reality. So if I just wholeheartedly trust him to do the right thing, he will. And if I don't trust him, he'll feel it, and it will make him do something bad. He'll become even more untrustworthy. So if I just keep trusting him, everything will be okay.*

Needless to say, those like Alicia who trust blindly and foolishly are the people who get burned the worst by life. If we get burned badly and often, we may abandon trust altogether.

Diligent distrust lies at the other end of the trust continuum. When we have been lied to, betrayed, disappointed, and abused, we can adopt an "I'll-never-trust-again" stance toward life. Karen adopted this stance after her husband drifted away and she reluctantly filed for divorce to end their seven-year marriage.

"Trust doesn't get you anywhere," Karen says bitterly. "I trusted Kevin, and look where it got me. I busted my butt for him and then he dumped me. Don't talk to me about trust. Look, I helped put him through graduate school, I was there for him during every crisis, I gave him encouragement to continue when he almost dropped out because he couldn't write his dissertation. And then — boom! — he's got his degree, got a job as an assistant professor of English, and he's off smoking dope, drinking, and screwing around with coeds. So he dumps me because I haven't grown enough, and I'm left with a kid, hit and miss child support, and a job as a secretary because I don't have my degree. Don't talk to me about trust."

Diligent distrust can take other forms. "Hey, I know there's a problem, I know I did some rotten things when I was heavy into alcohol and drugs," Colin says. "But give me a break. Jennifer's so paranoid, she can't hardly stand to let me out of her sight. She checks up on me constantly, calls me at work, keeps track of my time away from home right down to the minute. She goes through the pockets of my clothes like she's looking for something to incriminate me, a clue that I've been out partying. I tell her, 'Hey, lighten up, give me some slack.' But she gives me that look, like, you know, I don't deserve any slack. I mean, she's really backing me into a corner."

There is an alternative to credulity and suspicion. There is a way to become more trusting, a way to avoid the extremes of blind trust and utter distrust. We call it *vigilant trust* — a form of trust that can resolve some of the complications surrounding diligent distrust and blind trust.

Vigilant Trust

What is vigilant trust, and how does it differ from ordinary, common, garden-variety trust? We might say that *vigilant trust* is the quality of relying upon the integrity and fairness of people, while keeping our eyes peeled for danger. It's like saying, "Okay, I'll give this person a chance, but if I see danger signs I'm going to take action to protect myself."

When we are deciding whether or not to trust another person or situation, the most important information we have to help us make our decision is *history*. How has this person behaved in the past? What's his or her record of trustworthiness?

Some recovering people protest here. "That's not fair!" Manuel said. "In the past I was drunk all the time. Of course, I was untrustworthy."

Exactly. But Manuel, and other recovering people, are rebuilding their trust account right now. We are creating a new version of our personal history, a version that is marked by recovery, honesty, and reliability. But this new version of personal history covers only a short period. If we don't know anything about a person's track record, or if the record of sobriety is short, we really have no reason to be trusting.

Just because we feel honest and dependable now that we have a short period of recovery behind us doesn't mean we should expect other people to trust us or that we should even trust ourselves. Vigilant trust requires us to look at our own history. If we look at ourselves honestly, we'll see a fallible being, a person who many times has given in to temptation even when the will to resist was strong.

Willard found this out the hard way. He's a married man who works as a traveling sales representative. He's also a recovering alcoholic. "I've been trying to get sober for five years," Willard says. "I'd go a few months on the program, then there'd be a binge, then back on the program. I promised my wife I'd be faithful, and I meant it, but there've been a number of affairs with women I've picked up. And I might as well admit it, with prostitutes too."

Willard's now been sober for thirteen months, his longest period of sobriety ever. How's he doing it? "I finally admitted to myself that I was an untrustworthy son-of-a-gun and I had to stop putting myself in situations where I knew I couldn't be trusted. To be exact, I'm talking about bars and whorehouses."

While on the road, Willard used to check into a nice hotel, fully intending to stay sober and faithful to his wife. But he'd go into the cocktail lounge and order mineral water before dinner. Later, if he saw an attractive, unescorted woman he'd ask her to dance. And occasionally, he'd go with a group of other men to a brothel. "I'd say I was going as the designated driver," he explains. "The other guys would be drinking and .. . uh, visiting with the women . . . and I said I'd drink Pepsi and wait for them. I was a prince of a man, not wanting any of them to get busted for drunk driving."

Willard simply wasn't strong enough to hang around bars, alcohol, and willing women and still stay sober and monogamous. "Who was I kidding?" Willard asks. "A man doesn't go to a bar to drink mineral water and he doesn't go to a brothel to talk about drunk driving laws. I wasn't being vigilant with myself. I thought I was strong enough to resist temptation, but I'm not. As far as I'm concerned a man who wants to stay sober has no business in bars and if he wants to stay faithful to his wife, he's got no business cuddling up with a strange woman in a dark smoky corner. I mean, get real!"

When trust is an issue, we tend to think about other people's trustworthiness. While it's wise for us to be wary in our dealings with others, it's wiser still for us to heed our own shortcomings.

- Do we have trouble resisting chemicals? Then we need to get all alcohol and other drugs out of our house. We need to stay away from bars and parties and former friends who are still into drinking and drugs.
- Do we have a history of compulsive spending? Then we need to stay away from the mall, scissor our credit cards, and throw out all our mail-order catalogues.
- Do we have a history of sexual unfaithfulness? Then we

need to avoid putting ourselves into compromising situations with sexually attractive and available partners, other than the person to whom we are committed. With the threat of AIDS, sexual faithfulness is becoming more important than ever.

Vigilant Trust in Action

It takes time, sobriety, and unequivocal changes in behavior to rebuild trust.

The time factor varies for everyone. The early members of Alcoholics Anonymous knew that newfound sobriety was often fragile and that even staunch members of A.A. couldn't always be depended upon. In *Alcoholics Anonymous Comes of Age*, Bill Wilson gives a vivid example of vigilant trust. The Big Book of A.A. — *Alcoholics Anonymous* — was published in April 1939. It was the first complete statement of the A.A. philosophy, and members of the struggling young fellowship waited expectantly for a response from the public.

Unfortunately, very few people seemed interested in the book that promised so much for recovery from alcoholism. There were a few scattered reviews but no book orders, no real publicity about the promise of new hope for alcoholics. Bill W. notes, "Right through the summer of 1939 all attempts to get national magazines to print pieces about Alcoholics Anonymous failed."

Casting about for a way to get publicity for the book, one of the early A.A. members came up with a sure-fire idea. He explained his plan to his fellow recovering alcoholics: "I used to be in the ad business and had a great deal to do with radio. I know Gabriel Heatter very well, and I'm sure he would give us a hand." At that time, Gabriel Heatter was one of the foremost news commentators on national radio.

Gabriel Heatter agreed to publicize Alcoholics Anonymous and give The Big Book a plug on his "We, The People" radio program in a series of three-minute interviews with Morgan, an A.A. member.

As the date drew near for Morgan's appearance on national radio, other A.A. members became excited. And worried. Bill Wilson recalls, "With some of the past fiascoes in mind, somebody sounded a note of caution: What if the lately released asylum inmate Morgan should be drunk the day of the broadcast! Hard experience told us this was a real possibility. How could such a calamity be averted?"

Now here's a perfect example of vigilant trust in action. Morgan's friends gently suggested to him that they'd keep him under close surveillance until the night of the broadcast. Not merely under surveillance — *his friends proposed to lock him up.*

Morgan finally agreed, not without some resentment, and a double room was rented in the Downtown Athletic Club in New York. Morgan grumbled loudly, but agreed to become a willing captive, and for several days Bill Wilson and fellow A.A. members took turns staying with him around the clock, never letting him out of their sight.

The broadcast came off at the appointed hour. Bill Wilson remembers the immediate impact: "Sighs of relief went up in every New York member's home when Morgan's voice was heard. He had hit the deadline without getting drunk."

The broadcast was an historic occasion for A.A. And the precautions taken behind the scenes were vigilant trust in action.

When A.A. was still a fledgling organization, the members knew from experience that sobriety is sometimes fragile. They knew that under pressure even those most dedicated to sobriety can slip and fall off the wagon. They didn't want to take Morgan's word that he'd stay sober, because they knew that promises are easy to make and easy to break — they knew that alcoholism leaves a trail of broken promises. And Morgan knew it too. That's why he agreed to be locked up.

Promises — spoken and unspoken — and dependability form the basis of trust. And trust is the essential ingredient of all intimate relationships. Indeed, without trust, there would be no intimacy. Thus, intimacy requires us to be both trusting and *trustworthy* — to be able to trust and to be worthy of the trust others place in us.

Trust Builders

Sobriety, of course, is the number one trust-builder in relationships where alcohol and other drug abuse has been an issue. There can be no intimacy, no real trust, if both partners aren't clean and sober.

Decency is another trust-builder. This is an old-fashioned term that we don't hear much about anymore except in sermons decrying scantily clad females. But the dictionary gives the words "honest," "kind," "considerate," "proper," and "trustworthy" as synonyms for *decent*. When we behave decently, we are living by the basic rule of intimacy, that is, we act not only in our self-interest, but also in the interest of others. We are kind, considerate, and fair. And we will occasionally put up with inconvenience for the benefit of those we love.

Decent behavior makes us trustworthy only when we act with *consistency*. When we are consistent, our behavior conforms to a single set of principles or beliefs. In other words, a consistent person doesn't pat you on the back in the morning and stab you in the back in the afternoon. When we are consistent, our behavior becomes predictable.

To some people, the word *predictable* is synonymous with *boring*. And it's frequently true. When we behave with predictable decency, our lives lose a lot of excitement. There's no more heart-thumping agitation when one of our schemes is about to be uncovered. No more exhilaration as we outwit a suspicious partner. No more fever of dread as our house of lies topples around us. Instead, we are left with the boring predictability of sobriety, decency, and consistency. Many people find it a worthy trade.

Real Trust Issues

Instead of talking about trust as a grand abstract ideal, it's critical that couples address specific trust issues that arise between them. For instance,

- "I want to trust that you won't give me any sexually transmitted diseases."
- "I want to trust that you won't clean out the bank account and run off to Hawaii with a new lover."
- "I want to trust you to stay off drugs."
- "I want to trust you not to be overly critical, not to laugh at my mistakes, or find ways of making me feel small."

In other words, we must let our partner know what we expect — specifically — in the relationship, rather than depending on eloquent silences and ambiguous gestures to convey our thoughts and wishes.

We must recognize that to trust intelligently, we must be vigilant, for the truth is many people and situations are not worthy of our confidence. As the saying goes, "Just because we're paranoid doesn't mean they're not out to get us." If we are feeling emotionally starved, it is embarrassingly easy for us to be conned by smiling strangers.

Consider Mona, recovering from chemical dependency and herself the daughter of an alcoholic. Mona met a delightful man at a conference. They were both counselors. They sat next to each other through several presentations on intimacy and self-esteem and as the hours passed the vibrations seemed to grow and dance between them. *At last,* Mona thought, *a man who understands.*

They spent the night in his hotel room making passionate love. And the next day . . . he acted like he'd never met her before.

Mona was devastated. She had placed her trust in this seemingly warm and genuine stranger and he had used her, then tossed her aside.

The problem for many people, like Mona, whose lives have been conflicted by chemical dependency is not that they lack the ability to trust, but that *they trust indiscriminately*. They trust too quickly and they place their trust blindly. They may appear tough and cynical on the outside, but on the inside they are naive, easily conned, and overly eager to turn casual relationships into strong commitments.

Here's one of the great paradoxes of romance: We can be rejecting, doubting, and critical toward a mate or friend who has stood by our side through conflict and turmoil, yet we will willingly open our heart, soul, and body to a captivating liar whose charming demeanor is designed to make us feel special, if only for a moment. And then we wonder why we get burned.

In these times when we are urged to open ourselves up, to take risks, and to make ourselves vulnerable, we will also be wise to practice vigilance.

Trust does not require blind acquiescence. It requires prudence. The ability to think, to make rational judgments, and to accept people as they really are rather than how we would like them to be — these are the elements of vigilant trust.

CHAPTER EIGHT

Barrier #7: Sex

Alcoholics Anonymous says, "We all have sex problems. We'd hardly be human if we didn't." As usual, the founders of A.A. knew what they were talking about when it came to chemical dependency.

Sex can be a major area of difficulty — and a distressing barrier to intimacy — for recovering people. Why?

- Excessive use of alcohol and other drugs can physically hamper our ability to function sexually, causing impotence in men and loss of sexual response in women.

- Guilt. Perhaps we're ashamed of some of the sexual things we did while under the influence. Or maybe the only way we could work up the nerve to be sexual was by using alcohol or other drugs to overcome our inhibitions. As the saying goes, "The superego is soluble in alcohol."

- Fear can be a big obstacle too. Fear of sex. Fear of making a fool of ourselves, or fear of being used and hurt.

- Ignorance always plays a role when our sexuality is chaotically compulsive or pitifully nonexistent. Most of us never had any sex education, or if we did it was sanitized to the point of boredom. Or our sex education came from *Playboy*, *Penthouse*, and *Cosmopolitan*, hardly sources of realism. (Comedian Mort Sahl once quipped that a whole generation of American males, accustomed to the *Playboy* centerfold, came of age believing their Playmate would come equipped with a staple in her navel.)

Sex Talk: Uptight and Off Limits

In *The McGill Report on Male Intimacy*, Michael McGill writes, "Few issues are as volatile in marital relationships as the issue of sex — sexual identity, sexual satisfaction, sexual relationships. This volatility is largely latent, below the surface, often acted on and experienced by each partner, but rarely talked about."

Men and women alike frequently have the notion that sexual intimacy should come naturally in a loving relationship. Talking about sexual likes and dislikes, fantasies, desires, and so on, somehow takes the bloom off the rose — degrades sex, makes it dirty, disgusting, repugnant.

Sexuality can be the rawest area of a recovering person's self-esteem. In recovery meetings and therapy groups we're often encouraged to talk about our anger, our fear, or our depression, but sex remains a taboo topic for many people, even for some therapists. Most of the time, the subject of sex will simply be ignored, but sometimes recovering people will be actively discouraged from speaking out on sexual aspects of the recovery process.

Dennis found out about the sex taboo early in his recovery. Dennis is a laid-back, thirty-four-year-old divorced professional. He's tall, has a lean athletic build, and piercing, Paul Newman-blue eyes. He has the kind of smile that makes hearts flutter and orthodontists rich. He glitters when he walks. A corporate lawyer, Dennis earns good money, and has no trouble attracting women. "I've been what you might call a 'stud' since I was a teenager," Dennis says. "I was also an alcoholic and a drug addict. I'm sober and clean now, and I'm one grateful guy for my sobriety. But I'll tell you, recovery has played hell with my love life."

One night at a recovery meeting, Dennis started talking about some of the sexual complications that came up after he quit drinking. His words were met with an embarrassed silence. Finally, someone changed the subject.

After the meeting several men approached Dennis. "Listen, Dennis," one man said. "What you said tonight, we think it was . . . uh, you know — inappropriate. This meeting is for people with alcohol and drug problems, not — you know — *sex problems*. So maybe you better watch it in the future. Okay?"

Dennis agreed, but he felt really letdown. For him sex, alcohol, and other drugs were all tied up together in one package. He explains, "I started drinking when I was fifteen years old. I had sex for the first time when I was seventeen. It was great. I was drunk and so was the girl. It didn't take me long to figure out that the easiest way to get my date out of her panties was to get her drunk first. Then I met a girl I didn't have to coax. She liked drinking, drugs, and sex as much as I did. We got married when she was nineteen and I was twenty."

Marriage didn't mean settling down for Dennis and Mindy. They partied every weekend, smoked marijuana every day, started using cocaine on special occasions. By the time Dennis was thirty, he was a physical wreck. Dennis and Mindy divorced. Dennis remembers: "After Mindy and I broke up, I vowed I'd score with a different woman every weekend. I spent the next year in an alcohol- and drug-induced haze. I'd wake up with women I didn't recognize. It was totally crazy and it damn near killed me."

Dennis ended up in the hospital with severe hepatitis and pancreatitis. Dennis says, "The doctor told me flat out I could either quit the booze and drugs, or I could die. I asked him to help me, and that night he sent a couple of guys from A.A. to talk to me. I've been sober ever since."

Dennis regained his health. At age thirty-three, he found himself interacting with women without the aid of chemicals for the first time in his life. "It came as a real shock," he reflects, "when I realized that I'd never once made love sober. When I was high, I didn't care about anything. I didn't care what the woman thought of me because usually she didn't mean anything to me. It was all selfish, totally uncaring."

As intimate relationships with several women he was dating began to evolve, Dennis was confronted by challenges to his sexuality he had never thought about before. He was scared. "My ex-wife and I saw each other a few times and we ended up in bed together." Dennis shakes his head at the memory. "My first sober sex act with Mindy was a total disaster. I felt clumsy and awkward. I hadn't been with a woman in quite awhile. I started thinking, *What if I fail? What if I'm impotent? What if I'm too excited? What if I don't satisfy her?* It was all over real fast. Too fast. Mindy was not amused. She told me not to bother calling her again."

Dennis, who for years had considered himself a stud, now was suddenly overcome with sexual anxiety. "During my sobriety, I've faced all sorts of stress, with my job especially. Never once did I have the urge to deal with it by getting stoned. But with this sex thing, you know, there's been a couple of times when I started thinking, *What the hell? I don't want to be a monk the rest of my life. If drinking's the only way I can have a sex life, well then maybe just a little beer. . . .* You see what I mean? You see how crazy it is? For me, resolving my sexual anxiety is a vital part of my recovery program."

Men, Sex, and Recovery

McGill notes that men are even more silent and evasive about sexuality than women: "Research data illustrate that fewer than two out of every ten men have disclosed their favorite forms of sex play, their former sex partners, or their sexual fantasies, even to their wives." Men, says McGill, treat sexual issues as the most personal of personal information, the last data to be disclosed — if, indeed, it is disclosed at all.

And men are notoriously reluctant to talk about sexual problems. After all, men are supposed to be preoccupied with sex, horny, and instantly ready for sex. And men pride themselves on being great lovers. In our culture, real men don't have performance anxiety. Real men don't suffer from premature ejaculation. And certainly, real men aren't impotent.

Men can joke about sex. They can even appreciate the humor in someone else's sexual inadequacy, say, the pairing of George Burns and Gracie Allen. In *Gracie: A Love Story*, George Burns writes, "I have to be honest. I was a lousy lover. But Gracie married me for laughs, not for sex. Of course, she got both of them — when we had sex, she laughed."

It comes off nicely as a self-deflating quip — especially when told by a comedian who's in his nineties. But not many men would relish telling jokes about their own sexual inadequacies.

Performance anxiety, premature ejaculation, lack of interest in sex, impotence — these are the major sexual hang-ups men face during recovery. Negative thoughts and irrational attitudes intensify the hang-ups.

Not all sexual maladies stem from psychological causes. We know that depression, anxiety, fears and phobias, guilt, and shame can affect sexual functioning. But numerous other factors may cause sexual difficulties. Some of the causes of sexual dysfunction in men include:

- *Alcohol and street drugs* — often used to enhance sexual excitement, but can cause impotence, sexual indifference (sometimes called "loss of libido"), and delayed ejaculation.
- *Prescription medication* — drugs used to control hypertension can lead to decreased sex drive and certain forms of impotence. Steroids used by athletes to enhance athletic performance may have the opposite effect on sexual performance and can induce shrinking of the testicles. Tranquilizers, sleeping pills, painkillers, and antidepressants can delay or retard ejaculation.
- *Medical disorders* — a long list of diseases can interfere with sexual functioning: Hormonal disorders, heart, lung, and vascular diseases (such as congestive heart failure and emphysema), neurologic disorders (multiple sclerosis, cerebral palsy, or spinal cord tumor or trauma), liver or kidney

failure, obesity, lead or herbicide poisoning. All can contribute to impotence and other sexual disorders.

Because sexual problems may be caused or complicated by so many other factors, Dr. David Burns, author of *Intimate Connections*, suggests this sound advice:

> Anyone with a persistent sexual problem should seek professional consultation with a qualified clinic or physician specializing in sexual disorders so that the problem can be properly diagnosed and treated. There are many effective interventions, including education, medical and surgical treatments, individual psychotherapy, or couples therapy.

Sex as Intimacy: A Basic Conflict

For many men, sex and intimacy are inseparable. In effect, sex *is* intimacy. According to *The McGill Report*, one of the chief areas of sexual conflict and misunderstanding between men and women is the male tendency to link intimacy with sex. Men tend to feel that the sex act alone is sufficient evidence of intimacy, that sexual intercourse is the supreme expression of intimacy, and that nothing else is necessary to deal with sexual issues in a relationship.

As one woman told researchers on male intimacy, "Men only know one way to be sexy — screw. They can't understand that a woman wants some physical attention that doesn't always end up in the missionary position."

Another woman expressed her frustration: "I think being close means sharing. He thinks being close means screwing! . . . The whole idea of having an intimate relationship with someone, as far as I'm concerned, is being able to share your innermost feelings and emotions, not screw them away. When I'm anxious or insecure, I want to talk about it with someone who will listen — not just to what I'm saying, but to how I'm feeling too. When he's anxious or insecure, he wants sex; it reassures him."

When she comes home tired and tense from work, she wants to talk about the emotional garbage she's had to deal with. "When he comes home tired and tense, he wants me to 'do him' — you can guess what that means. Getting off is his tension release."

When she feels like she accomplished something, she wants to share her elation. When he has something special to celebrate, he expects "special sex" as his reward.

When she's sad, she gets a lot of consolation from having a shoulder to cry on and someone who will be empathetic. When he's sad, he wants to be seduced out of his sadness.

When she's mad, she wants to get it out in the open, let him know how she feels and why. She wants to fight. When he's mad, he wants to make love. He thinks that sex will solve everything, make up for whatever's wrong. "That's why I say the difference between me and my husband is that I want to share and he wants to screw."

She sums up: "He seems to think that if he's sharing his body, he's sharing himself. He doesn't understand that there are other ways to be loving without making love, or if he does understand, he doesn't do anything about it."

Many men make the mistake of thinking they can become more sharing and loving by taking a crash course in sexual physiology and techniques of lovemaking. The more important issues are the *attitudes and feelings* underlying male sexuality.

Clearly, more knowledge about sexual behavior and more attention to a partner's needs can greatly enhance a relationship. But be certain of this: Finding the G-spot or experimenting with a variety of sexual caresses and positions won't contribute to intimacy if feelings of affection, caring, and consideration are false, forced, or absent. The facts of physiology might be interesting and intellectually enlightening, and the techniques might be titillating, but they have nothing to do with the *experience* of sex — the felicitous caring and sharing of sex with a loving partner.

Sex and the Recovering Woman

"I had one big fear when I was in treatment for my alcoholism," said Barbara, a stocky brunette in her late thirties. "I dreaded going home and sleeping in the same bed with my husband, Mike."

It's not that Barbara disliked her husband. She loved him. But to Mike, marriage meant sex more than anything else. And he let Barbara know he'd dreamed up some very special events to celebrate her homecoming.

She wasn't interested. In fact, she had every intention of rejecting Mike's romantic advances. "I detested the thought of having sex with him," she said. "For twelve years I'd taken care of his needs, burying my resentments in a bottle. Now that I was sober, I couldn't bear the thought of meeting his demands."

Is Barbara an icy oddball, a woman so warped by sexual hang-ups that she'll never be able to carry on a loving relationship with a man? Is she different from other women struggling to overcome chemical dependency?

Not according to Jean, a recovering woman who counsels other women in the process of recovery. "For many women," says Jean, "the problem was sexual all along. Sex therapy should be part of a woman's treatment," she says, "because sex is the most predominant problem we see in recovering women."

Sexual Abuse

Many chemically dependent women have a history of sexual abuse and exploitation. We're not just talking about women who have endured loutish husbands. We're talking about rape, incest, and brutality.

Although there are no national statistics on the subject, many chemical dependency counselors estimate that nearly 50 percent of their female clients report having been sexually abused as children and teenagers.

Sexual abuse, experts agree, is especially damaging to a woman's feelings of self-worth. "When a woman is the victim of sexual abuse," explains Marion S., the program coordinator for a woman's treatment center, "society forces her to bear the guilt and stigma for what happened. She feels helpless, certain she's no good, an awful person, and thus, fair game for the demands of any man."

Helen, a thirty-seven-year-old nurse working on her first year of sobriety, had been sexually abused by her stepfather when she was a teenager. "Secretly, men terrified me," she admits, "but I learned early that a sweet smile and emotional passiveness protected me from male anger. So I went along with whatever men wanted. My sexual escapades didn't bother me when I was drinking, but I'd wake up with overwhelming feelings of guilt. My life became a great big vicious circle. I'd drink to get rid of my inhibitions, to please my man. Then in the morning I hated myself so much, I'd drink more to numb my feelings. I thought I must be the worst person in the world!"

Helen had never learned to respond to men as friends or even people. They were powerful beings to be appeased, pacified, and feared, but never to be trusted. Therapists who work with women who have been sexually abused say these women tend to be fearful of intimacy, or they may be clinging and overly dependent. They've never learned to respond to men appropriately.

Sexual Repression, Conflicting Images

Sexual abuse is one crucial factor blocking complete recovery from chemical dependency. Sexual repression, arising from conflicting images of a woman's role in the family and society is another.

In our society, women are expected to be the caregivers, putting the needs of the men in their lives and their children ahead of their own. Women, as wives and mothers, often neglect and fail to share their sexual desires and needs for support and intimacy. Yet, when a woman enters chemical dependency treatment she is given a vastly different and conflicting message: You have to start taking care of your own needs. You have to put yourself first. Your sobriety depends on it.

This double whammy can hit a recovering woman hard. Lois, who's been sober for three years, speaks from experience. "In the first five years of our marriage, my husband's needs always came before my own. I thought that was the way marriage was supposed to be. His job was to support me and my job was to make him happy. It was Jim first and me second. That included our sex life too. The sex was for him; my feelings didn't seem to count. I tried to drink my resentments and unhappiness away. Well, that didn't work."

When she came out of treatment she felt like a complete failure, as a wife and as a woman. "I felt totally unloved and worthless and couldn't see how my husband could like me, much less love me. But I desperately wanted to feel loved. I wanted us to be friends again. I wanted to be more than a warm body in bed beside him. When I tried to tell Jim how I felt, he acted like I'd gone crazy."

When Lois threatened divorce, Jim agreed to family counseling. "We never would have made it if I hadn't agreed to counseling too." he recalls. "At first, I thought the problem was entirely her's, but it was both of us. Our sex life still isn't all I'd like it to be, but we're working on it together. And you know, sex is better when both people are enjoying it."

What Lois wanted was for her husband to put her needs first for a change. This reversal in roles caused a terrible strain on their relationship.

In a fit of anger one night, Jim screamed at her, "I liked you better when you were drinking! At least then, you tried to please me."

It took time and many sessions with a marriage counselor, but Jim and Lois discovered there is a balance point between selfishness and self-sacrifice. "I no longer look at sex as my right," Jim says.

Lois adds, "And I no longer see it as my duty."

Women Without Partners

Almost all treatment programs recognize the need for both partners to enter treatment if the relationship is to be healed. But what about single, divorced, and widowed women — women without partners? How do they deal with their sexuality and intimacy needs after sobriety?

Too often the subject is ignored. Dana, a thirty-year-old divorcee, went through a three-week inpatient program in a reputable hospital. Sexuality was touched on briefly during one film, then ignored for the rest of treatment. "My counselor was a man," she says. "He was attentive and gave me the feeling he was really interested in me as a person, so we talked about a lot of things. But — well, you know how it is. And there were six men in my treatment group. I certainly wasn't going to talk about my most intimate secrets in front of them!"

But Dana needed to talk about her sex life because, by her own admission, men were her biggest problem, next to alcohol. "When I was drinking,"she says, blushing, "I found myself in some pretty raunchy situations. I'd wake up with strangers! Two strangers!"

When she quit drinking, her wildest sexual exploits ceased. Instead, she entered into a series of "steady" romances with men who sometimes treated her cruelly and who did not respect her hard-earned sobriety. She admits, "I used myself as bait for every loser in town."

Counselors who work with recovering women are only too familiar with the self-destructive course taken by the recovering woman who has not yet salvaged her self-esteem. As one counselor puts it: "Loneliness and insecurity can lead a woman into a 'fatal attraction' to men who are not good for her. Often he is a drinking alcoholic himself." She adds, "A relationship with an alcoholic man is just like a time bomb ready to go off."

Dana learned the hard way. By accepting dates with heavy-drinking men, she exposed herself again to the bar life and its temptations. "I fell off the wagon with a resounding crash. Luckily, I finally sobered myself up and got back into treatment. This time I'm staying away from the bars and men who drink and who think a woman is good for only one thing, because when I'm with those men I hate them and I hate myself."

Dana is right. Suffering and guilt-ridden women must admit the mammoth proportions of their self-hatred and self-disgust before they can begin to deal with emotional and sexual isolation.

Recovering women must talk about their shame and guilt and anger before they can heal. Yet, many women are reluctant to do so. Marion bluntly sums up her counseling experience: "A woman won't talk about what's really bothering her if there's a man in the room. The whole alcoholism community is just beginning to recognize this — that women need the care and support of other women."

For Women Only

Some counselors advocate involvement in "women only" groups to help build an identity with other women. "Recovering women don't have an image of themselves as individuals," Jean says. In her counseling groups, she sees four common problems in recovering women: Poor self-esteem, depression, guilt, and sexual conflict. "They have no self-esteem, no self-value. They need to learn and commit to memory these messages to their inner self: *You are competent. You are capable.* But even more, they need to cultivate competence, they need to *be* capable, not just mouth fine-sounding affirmations. This sense of a competent, capable self can be an enormous help to improve sexual relations."

Julie, a new member of Women for Sobriety, agrees: "I went through inpatient treatment and I still attend A.A. meetings. Those things got me sober, but they didn't deal with the problems I have as a woman. I didn't feel comfortable talking about my most intimate fears in front of a group of men. I tried it a few times, and after the meetings a couple of the guys came on to me. I just wasn't ready for that. But when I'm with other women, I can really let my hair down. And they understand! For the first time I don't feel like some terrible misfit."

Recovering Self-Esteem

In our society, it's common for a woman to base her self-worth on the distorted reflection she sees in a man's eyes. She thinks if a man finds her sexually desirable, then she must have value.

Yet, a sexual relationship, with its inherent emotional entanglements, can cause more problems than it solves when a woman is trying to establish her identity as a separate and worthy individual.

Nicole, sober for five years, recommends that a newly sober woman concentrate on building up her self-esteem and confidence before building up her sex life: "There's time, believe me, plenty of time for sex. At first, a woman needs to learn to value herself. A sexual involvement might take energy away from the important rebuilding of ego. If a woman can't love herself, how can she truly love a man?"

She adds: "My advice is to put sex on the back burner for a while."

Jean agrees, suggesting that a woman wait six months to a year after beginning recovery before she even tries to establish a sexual relationship with a man.

Rebuilding Relationships

But what's a woman who has an established sex partner supposed to do with him while she's building her ego? Frank, a forty-year-old salesman, feels his experience is worth sharing with other men. "When my wife completed inpatient treatment, I thought all our problems were over. But emotionally, she was still in a million pieces, confused, frightened, yet very determined. She'd resented the way I sometimes treated her, resented it for years, but instead of confronting me openly, she'd take it out on me in bitchy ways totally unrelated to the real problem. Burned dinners, a messy house, headaches, and, of course, the drinking. She didn't want to live like that anymore."

In treatment, Frank's wife attended classes in assertiveness. "She talked to me honestly for the first time, opening herself up emotionally to me like she'd never done before. It was a painful process for both of us. I'd always considered myself a skilled lover. It floored me when she said I was clumsy and selfish and she'd been faking her orgasms!"

Frank was dumbfounded. He felt like he'd been married to a stranger all these years. But after the shock wore off, and after some extraordinarily painful soul-searching, he agreed to participate in sex therapy. "We've learned a lot more than just techniques too. Now after all these years of marriage, we've learned to communicate our needs to each other. It hasn't been easy, but it's been worth it."

Elaine's husband wasn't willing to make that sort of effort. He left her shortly after she sobered up. "I was devastated," she says. "My first impulse was to run right out to snag another man." After two horrible one-night stands, she changed her mind. "I realized I didn't enjoy sex," she confides. "I used it as a weapon to manipulate men."

She started wondering if maybe she wasn't missing something. "Here I was, a thirty-five-year-old divorcee, I'd been with a half dozen different men in my life, and I'd never had an orgasm. And although I'd been hopelessly in love at times, I'd never really liked a man. I wanted to change that."

Sexual Healing

Some therapists suggest that women like Elaine start the healing process by learning about their own bodies and feelings. Well-known and informative books like the *Hite Reports*, *Our Bodies, Our Selves*, and *The Joy of Sex*, counteract fear that sexual feelings are abnormal or strange.

One therapist is blunt about what needs to be learned. "A woman should treat herself sensuously, take bubble baths, learn how to treat her body as if it is her lover. She should learn to masturbate to orgasm so she can tell her lover how to please her."

To some this may sound like unconventional advice, but those who recognize the anguish of the recovering woman's sexual conflict will not be as quick to condemn. It is encouraging to note that many women find true intimacy and sexual satisfaction as a pleasant side-benefit to the hard work leading to the rebuilding of a sober life and a healthy self-image.

How long this process takes varies from woman to woman. Some never heal. But the woman who has begun the task of restructuring her tattered self-esteem often develops a new openness and honesty that can foster caring emotional and sexual relationships.

The man who discovers such a woman may have little luck in bending her to his whims, but he very possibly will be much happier than the men who used to push her around.

For Recovering Men *and* Women

One of the most important steps recovering men and women can take to surmount sexual barriers to intimacy is this: Learn to respect the emotional and sexual vulnerability of other recovering people. And try not to compensate for anxiety over real or imagined sexual inadequacy by becoming a sexual predator. Translation: Don't use recovery groups to seek out sexual partners.

And keep in mind that sexual behavior cannot be isolated

from other aspects of a relationship. Sex may be wonderful and even mind-boggling at times, but as one recovering woman said with tongue in cheek, "Remember, you've got to think about what you're going to be doing with each other the other twenty-three hours and fifty-seven minutes of the day."

CHAPTER NINE

Barrier #8: Romance Versus Reality

> By Chivalries as tiny,
> A Blossom, or a Book,
> The seeds of smiles are planted—
> Which blossom in the dark.
> — Emily Dickinson

In romantic fiction, love conquers all. No tiny chivalries here — in the Realm of Romance, the action is much more swash-buckling and dramatic. The hero and heroine need only gaze into each other's eyes and suddenly a primal awareness erases misunderstanding, conflict, and doubt. The heroine's defenses melt under the fire of the hero's piercing gaze and masterful kisses. Locked in each other's arms, the lovers soar to the ultimate heights of intimate ecstasy. There is a raw electricity, thunder in the blood, and the sound of wild, wind-ravaged waves dashing on the rocks below. And later, in the afterglow, they share a low-tar cigarette.

As the story goes, they live happily ever after.

Meanwhile, back in the real world, many recovering women and men find intimate relationships are not fulfilling their most deeply felt needs. There are more rotten socks than there are roses. There's a dearth of dahlias and an abundance of dirty underwear. Passionate kisses, if they come at all, don't erase the lingering resentments, don't compensate for loneliness, and don't end the power struggles typical of relationships scarred by chemical dependency.

Yet the notion of perfect intimacy persists. A yearning, a longing for a blissful union.

Happily Ever After

The Romantic Ideal can be seen in what novelist Trish Vradenburg calls the "happily-ever-after conditioning" we get as we grow up. In *Liberated Lady*, Vradenburg tells the story of a thirty-eight-year-old divorcee, Jessica Kantor. After her divorce from her physician-husband, Jess swore off men. She had gotten burned once and was going to make certain it didn't happen again. She summed up her feelings about relationships with men: "Scrape away the layers, the core is just the same. I'll never expose myself to that pain again."

So Jess concentrated her energies on her career and her daughter and became known as the "Iron Lady" administrative assistant of a powerful U.S. Senator. But from time to time even the Iron Lady yearned for romance:

> For all she had sworn off men when she and Eliot split for good, Jess still had a lingering fantasy that some prince on a white steed would spot her unloading her Shoprite groceries, fall madly in love, scoop her up, and gallop back to his castle (anywhere on Park Avenue was acceptable).
>
> Happily-ever-after conditioning, she realized, was hard to break.

The notion of life being Happy Ever After comes, of course, from fairy tales — the stories we were told as children where young lovers triumphed over wickedness and lived happily ever after. Snow White and Cinderella are rescued by a Prince Charming. It makes a nice story, but it can get you into trouble if you look forward to being rescued from a life of care and worry by a Prince Charming who will make everything better.

This kind of fairy tale continues to be told in movies. In *The Pick-Up Artist*, the hero saves his young lady from her father (a practicing alcoholic) and from evil gangsters by winning enough money at Atlantic City to pay off the bad guys (the Lottery Mentality). Love prevails. The movie ends on that high note, with the implicit message: *And they lived happily ever after.*

But the young couple had only known each other for two days. The same day the hero (a pick-up artist, so-called because he specialized in picking up beautiful women on the streets of New York) picked up his True Love, he drove her to a park where they had sex in the front seat of the car. Pretty good sex, from the sound of it, even though it was daylight and the risk of discovery was high.

Now that's the first date.

The point is this: True love just doesn't happen like that. Even the truest of true loves must take place in a world where ordinary folks eat and sleep, work and play, thrive and fail.

Romantic Repercussions

One aspect of the Romantic Ideal that can lead to trouble is the belief that we can and should be able to make our partner happy all the time and our partner should be able to do the same for us. When problems crop up, as inevitably they will, we can end up feeling inadequate or betrayed. For example, when the stress of family life and job pressures built up, Thelma, who in many ways is a competent and capable woman, began fantasizing about someone taking care of her. Her husband, Jack, seemed inadequate when compared with Thelma's Romantic Ideal. This is the way Thelma put it: "I alternated between fantasies of winning the lottery and meeting some wonderful, rich man who would fall madly in love with me. I felt my life was out of control. I was terribly disappointed in Jack because he didn't seem to be doing anything to solve our problems. I wanted someone who could just make the problems go away."

Jack, of course, couldn't make all the problems go away. And Thelma's romantic fantasies turned into bitterness and resentment.

As more women have moved out of the home and into the work force, they have also felt freer to demand the rights and freedoms that come with economic independence. Yet, a very normal and natural desire to be protected and cared for remains. Under these circumstances, a woman can feel trapped and resentful.

Rose confided her romantic fantasies to her therapist: "When I married Jim, I thought we'd be the local version of Sleeping Beauty and Prince Charming — all romance and tenderness and consideration for each other. But sometimes he's just so . . . *irritating*. Instead of being like Prince Charming, he acts like *Elmer Fudd*. I ended up being terribly disappointed in him, but I didn't dare say anything, because I didn't want to hurt his feelings."

Rose isn't disappointed just in Jim. Like many others who grew up in stressful, insecure homes, she gets terribly down on herself when she doesn't measure up to the perfect person she would like to be.

She believes that if she were that perfect person, she would somehow be able to make Jim into the man she wants him to be. If he acts upset or depressed or unhappy, she feels guilty and blames herself. She believes it's up to her to solve the problems in their marriage, and she thinks that if she only works a little harder and gets Jim to change a little more, everything will be better.

Although she's unhappy with Jim's behavior, she finds it difficult to tell him how she feels and what she really wants from him. So Jim has to go around guessing about why Rose is irritable and defensive toward him. Because she doesn't want to hurt his feelings or start a fight, she keeps her worries inside rather than expressing them openly.

Naturally this strategy doesn't work. She ends up tense and

annoyed, and although Jim doesn't know what the problem is, Rose's lack of enthusiasm and her hangdog look tell Jim loud and clear: I'm dissatisfied with you.

In the early years of their marriage, when they had extra money and a lot of leisure time, they were able to ignore the underlying tension between them. But after the baby came, when extra money and leisure time were almost nonexistent, the pressure built to the breaking point.

So there they are — Rose feels betrayed and angry because Jim's not living up to her expectations and Jim feels rejected and insecure. And neither of them will talk about it directly.

Everyday Life: A Banal Barrier to Intimacy

When we think about barriers to intimacy, we most commonly focus on relationship problems, interpersonal problems, barriers to intimacy that arise when communication falters or fails. We detect clues of diminished trust and watch the distance grow between us until there is nothing left for us, not even the cold comfort of a chilly togetherness.

How then do we view everyday life as a barrier to intimacy? Let's look at what some couples envisage as a perfect life in the suburbs. The cosmetic image of the suburban ideal conceals the somewhat blemished reality:

- Our visions of carefree home ownership don't include the realities of sizable long-term mortgages, escalating real estate taxes and utility bills, and recurring repair costs.
- The suburban life usually entails a commute on crowded highways or on public transportation teeming with others who have sought the carefree suburban existence. The trip has become increasingly time-consuming, tedious, nerve-racking, wretched, and at times vicious and even fatal.
- The job can be a haven, but not a very safe and secure one, because of the prospect of layoffs, mergers, cost-cutting, and transfers to new locations.

- There is the joy of parenthood, true. And there are also the responsibilities that come with a long-term commitment to parenthood. There are childhood diseases to contend with, finding good schools (and not having the luxury to afford the finest), constraints on time, and the problem of finding good, reliable babysitters. And then there's the storm and stress of adolescence. . . .

- Even for couples with no children, everyday life generates many unforeseen complications — in employment status, unexpected downturns in cash flow, relocation, and other stresses that strain relationships to the breaking point. That's the reality beneath the diaphanous surface of the Romantic Ideal.

Psychologist Arnold Lazarus, judged to be one of the ten most influential therapists in America in an *American Psychologist* survey, contends that most couples enter marriage with impossible expectations. His book, *Marital Myths*, is a collection of two dozen marital myths — impossible expectations that undermine relationships.

Lazarus writes: "Marriage is not a romantic interlude; it is a practical and serious relationship." It requires tangible evidence of conjugal caring and affection: Kindness, consideration, communication, harmonious adjustment to each other's habits, and clear evidence of mutual respect. This kind of love fosters tiny chivalries — an unexpected simple gift, doing a task unasked to please one's partner, taking the time to share a cup of coffee and watch the chickadees and the finches fluttering around a bird feeder.

What are some of the basic requirements in a practical relationship? Says Lazarus, "Married couples must adjust to daily routines of dressing, eating, working, sleeping and similar habits that call for synchronous schedules. . . . The aim is to build up a 'common capital' of acts, habits and experiences that result in a profound acceptance of each other, without the false hopes and impossible illusions of the romantic ideal."

Spencer and Kate Muddle Through

"I shudder when I think of it now," Kate says. "It was a nightmare that neither one of us anticipated — not in our wildest dreams. Looking back, I think it's a wonder Spencer and I muddled through. So much of the stress we experienced at that time was out of our control. The job market was zilch all over the country. Housing was hard to get. If it had lasted much longer, I don't know whether we would have survived as a couple."

Here's what happened: Several years ago, Spencer lost his job due to a cutback in state funds that came as a result of state-wide tax reform. Ironically, Spencer had worked for nine years as a job counselor for the state employment division. "Suddenly, there I was, supposedly an expert in helping people find jobs, and I had to live on unemployment for about six months."

Kate took his unemployment gracefully for a while. But she soon found herself getting angry. "I couldn't believe that Spencer couldn't find a job. It was embarrassing because I had the feeling my friends and even my family thought Spencer wasn't really trying. After all, he had a terrific work record."

Was it because of his history of alcoholism? There had been some job problems five or six years ago, but Spencer had taken advantage of the Employee Assistance Program at work and had gone through treatment. His work record since then was exemplary. But still the nagging thought remained: *Am I branded or red-tagged as an incorrigible, screwed-up alcoholic?*

Kate, a legal secretary, went to work one day and discovered that the attorneys she worked for had invested in a fast-buck mortgage company that went bankrupt. There would be no more need for her services. She took it in stride because she knew she was skilled, but when she started looking for work, Kate found the established lawyers had sufficient help, and the young lawyers — who were graduating from law schools in hungry, highly competitive wolf packs — couldn't afford to hire top-notch legal secretaries. They could get their briefs typed at a secretarial service for a dollar a page.

Kate, looking at the prospect of having to work as a typist for minimum wage, quickly got a new perspective on Spencer's employment struggle.

Meanwhile, Spencer did find work at last. He got a job in a mill. "I hadn't done any physical labor for years, and then all of a sudden I was looking at a ten-hour shift stacking lumber for a forklift loader. It was mindless, endless, backbreaking work. The noise from the saws was deafening, but the company didn't provide any earplugs. I finally wadded up some paper and plugged my ears. All this for $4.25 an hour. I tell you, I almost wept with relief when my first ten-hour shift ended and the foreman told me that the shift was being laid off indefinitely because of overstocked inventory."

When their bank account was near zero, in desperation Spencer picked up an out-of-town newspaper and applied for a job as the manager for a halfway house for recovering alcoholics. "With my own treatment and experience in A.A., and my background in psychology and job counseling, I figured I'd be a cinch for the job."

"Whither thou goest, I will follow," Kate said lightly. But she wasn't keen on the idea. It meant pulling up roots, leaving old friends and family members, moving to a new community. But still it was a new chance for Spencer.

"It was an immediate disaster," Kate recalls. "We couldn't find a house or even an apartment to rent in the town where Spencer worked, so we finally located a rental in a country village about twenty-five miles away. No carpets, just cold linoleum on the floor. It took two weeks to get a telephone installed. And it rained every day for six months."

Kate went cabin crazy because she couldn't get out. They only had one car — and Spencer used it to commute to work. There was no public transportation, not even a taxi service.

The unpaved road that led to their rental home turned into a black clay mud bog, making walking difficult and daunting.

She couldn't find a job, and even when she went job hunting, it meant going into town with Spencer and being stuck all day with little or nothing to do.

They didn't have a television set. And the only heat was from a small electric heater. It took Spencer a week to figure out how to start a fire in the wood stove without smoking up the house, and by then the meager supply of dry wood was gone. It took him another week to locate someone who'd deliver a cord of wood — which turned out to be half usable, half waterlogged oak which was too large to fit in the stove and too knotty to split with an ax.

"I went cabin crazy," Kate says. "No phone, no TV, no friends or family to talk with. I read a lot of Nero Wolfe and Perry Mason. And I started nagging Spencer immediately when he got home from work — I was so anxious and upset. My life was hell, and I blamed him for every excruciating minute of it."

Fortunately, after about six weeks of this miserable existence, the cook at the halfway house told Spencer about a house that was going to be available, and Spencer and Kate were able to move from their clammy county hovel into town.

"Kate quickly found a job," says Spencer, "and we lived happily ever after."

Kate makes a wry face. "Well, almost. But one thing is certain — it never got that bad again. And whenever I get really dissatisfied with our relationship, I can look back to that rotten time as being the absolute low point in our lives. I mean if we got through that together, I figure we can get through just about anything."

What was the critical element that helped them weather the hard times? Was it love? Kate laughs. "I think it was tenacity. And hope. After all, we'd had a pretty good life together before the hard times set in, so we both sort of took it for granted that we could recapture a good life together. But keep in mind we both also kept working to make things better. We reduced our standard of living. We learned to be frugal. We didn't drift and we didn't just sit around dreaming and wishing for things to get better."

Beyond Wishful Thinking

Francine Klagsbrun has written insightfully about people who stay together in the age of divorce. In her book *Married People: Staying Together in the Age of Divorce*, Klagsbrun outlines eight main characteristics found in couples who are able to keep marriages together:

- Couples not only tolerate changing circumstances, but also have the ability to change, to make necessary adjustments, to roll with the punches.
- Couples learn to live with the unchangeable — with unresolved conflict, if necessary. (The essence of maturity, says Klagsbrun, is the ability to live with the imperfect.)
- Couples who stay together assume that marriage is for keeps. They show commitment to the relationship and to the institution of marriage. They do not have the attitude that marriage is a passing fancy, a temporary stop on the fast-lane express of serial monogamy.
- Couples trust each other. This trust involves mutual nurturance and protection, with the implicit assumption that there will be no ridicule or violation of the core issues of either partner.
- There is a balance of power in the relationship. This means that partners acknowledge their mutual dependencies, the emotional and economic contributions that each partner contributes to the relationship. When partners work out a balance of power, there is a sense that both are worthy mates.
- Couples who stay together *enjoy each other*, taking pleasure in being together, talking with each other, keeping each other company. They have shared values. This does not

mean total togetherness, but it does mean a readiness to share interests.

- They have a shared history, cherished memories that they use to build a sense of permanence, even inevitability, in their relationship. This mutual past becomes a kind of community memory, with code words, rituals, and private jokes. There's an enormously complicated shared history behind this simple exchange between a husband and his wife:

"Okay, where did you hide it?"
"Hide what?"
"You know."
"Where do you think?"
"Oh."

- And finally, couples must have a certain amount of luck — luck in choosing a mate who has the capacity to change and trust and love, luck in the family you come from, luck with life.

If so much depends on luck, then it seems as if our efforts in creating and maintaining relationships are virtually useless. Not so. As we indicated in our book, *Strong Choices, Weak Choices,* we can measurably enhance recovery by the strong choices we make. *We are not always powerless to control our luck.*

When we see couples who seem to be luckier than average, if we look closely enough, we'll find that they made strong choices in their relationship. They choose to make the most of the blessings of their own marriage, instead of yearning for the mythical ideal relationship. They don't deny difficulties in their own union, but they choose to find ways to smooth over the rough spots, ways to compromise.

Those who make strong choices always grab luck by the tail and twist it to their own purposes.

The Distinguished Stranger Strategy

Klagsbrun found many styles of relating among long-married couples. And this is perhaps her most significant discovery: *There is no magic formula for a stable, satisfying relationship.* No one style of relating was superior to any other style of relating, as long as each couple felt their own style was satisfactory.

William J. Lederer and Don D. Jackson reached a similar conclusion in *The Mirages of Marriage.* Reviewing the elements of a satisfactory marriage, Lederer and Jackson stress the importance of mutual respect, tolerance, and negotiation.

One key element: Partners recognize that a relationship is a process involving constant change. "And constant change," Lederer and Jackson insist, "requires the spouses to *keep working on their relationship until the day they die.*"

The alternative, of course, is to become a Gruesome Twosome.

According to Lederer and Jackson, companionability and respect — not love and romance — are the key words couples use to describe happy marriages. The happy, workable, productive marriage does not require a diet of love and romance: "Normal people should not be frustrated or disappointed if they are not in a *constant* state of love." What's the formula, then? Lederer and Jackson suggest that durable marriages can be formed when partners experience the joy of love (or imagine they do) for 10 percent of the time and when they treat each other with as much courtesy as they do distinguished strangers. It also helps when partners attempt to make the marriage a union where there are some practical advantages and satisfactions for each.

Perhaps the formula for a good relationship is in the end nothing more than this:

> *Pay attention to the tiny chivalries and small considerations, and be as courteous and respectful to your partner as you would be to a distinguished stranger.*

References & Notes

Chapter One

Page

13 *Victorian Murderesses*, Mary S. Hartman, New York: Schocken Books, 1977, 245.

Chapter Three

38 *Alcoholics Anonymous*, New York: Alcoholics Anonymous World Services, Inc., Second Edition, 1955, 62.

39 *Alcoholics Anonymous*, New York: Alcoholics Anonymous World Services, Inc., Second Edition, 1955, 62.

42 *Alcoholics Anonymous*, New York: Alcoholics Anonymous World Services, Inc., Second Edition, 1955, 69.

Chapter Four

53 *Alcoholics Anonymous*, New York: Alcoholics Anonymous World Services, Inc., Second Edition, 1955, 71.

55 *Feelings: Our Vital Signs*, Willard Gaylin, New York: Ballantine Books, 1979, 4.

56 *Alcoholics Anonymous*, New York: Alcoholics Anonymous World Services, Inc., Second Edition, 1955, 74

Chapter Five

67   *Love, Medicine & Miracles,* Bernie S. Siegel, M.D., New York: Harper & Row Publishers (Perennial Library), 1988, 179.

Chapter Seven

95   Story related in *Alcoholics Anonymous Comes of Age,* New York: Alcoholics Anonymous World Services, Inc., 1957, 172-75.

Chapter Eight

101   *Alcoholics Anonymous,* New York: Alcoholics Anonymous World Services, Inc., Second Edition, 1955, 69.

102   *The McGill Report on Male Intimacy,* Michael E. McGill, New York: Holt, Rinehart & Winston, 1985, 251. McGill also notes:

> The reason that so many men experience a sense of meaningless is that they do not have loving connections with others who would give meaning to their lives and their actions. In the absence of a caring relational context, a man behaves in a vacuum. He doesn't care about his behavior because he doesn't care enough about others to value their caring. He collects achievements in life, but there is no caring context to give his efforts meaning. It's not unlike those family hand-me-downs, the bric-a-brac that litter our homes. An old tin cup, a cracked pickle dish, a faded photograph — they are unattractive, don't really fit in with the decor of the room. They have no value to anyone else, but they are priceless to us. Their meaning lies in the fact that they mean something to those who owned them before us. Without loving relationships, a man's life resembles bric-a-brac that has no history, no caring context, and hence no value.

104 *The McGill Report on Male Intimacy*, Michael E. McGill, New York: Holt, Rinehart & Winston, 1985, 58.

105 Quote by George Burns in *People Magazine*, 31 October 1988, 60 (cited from his book *Gracie: A Love Story*, New York: Putnam Publishers Group, 1988).

106 *Intimate Connections*, David Burns, M.D., New York: New American Library (Signet), 1985, 227.

106 *The McGill Report on Male Intimacy*, Michael E. McGill, New York: Holt, Rinehart & Winston, 1985, 189-90.

Chapter Nine

117 *The Complete Poems of Emily Dickinson*, Thomas H. Johnson, ed., Boston: Little, Brown & Co., 1960, 30.

118 *Liberated Lady*, Trish Vradenburg, New York: Dell Publishing, 1986, 150.

122 *Marital Myths: Two Dozen Mistaken Beliefs That Can Ruin a Marriage (Or Make a Bad One Worse)*, Arnold A. Lazarus, San Luis Obispo, Calif.: Impact Publishers, 1985, 168.

126 *Married People: Staying Together in the Age of Divorce*, Francine Klagsbrun, New York: Bantam Books, 1985, 296.

128 *The Mirages of Marriage*, William J. Lederer and Don D. Jackson, New York: W. W. Norton & Company, 1968, 59, 198-99.

Other books by Mark Worden and
Gayle Rosellini that will interest you...

Strong Choices, Weak Choices
The Challenge of Change in Recovery
Here is a healthy and constructive approach to making choices—and changes—in our lives. This lively, very readable book offers strategies for meeting the challenges that are sure to arise as we seek a healthier, happier, and more peaceful path through recovery. 145 pp.
Order No. 5037

Of Course You're Angry
Feeling angry is a normal, healthy emotion. Yet learning to express anger appropriately can be difficult. This book looks at many forms of anger such as violence, depression, and manipulation, and offers specific guidelines for learning healthy ways to acknowledge and express anger. 92 pp.
Order No. 1169

Here Comes the Sun
Dealing with Depression
Depression is a baffling and cunning disorder that can strike anyone, especially those of us recovering from alcoholism and other addictions. *Here Comes the Sun* is a hopeful, upbeat, and optimistic guide to recovery from depression. 224 pp.
Order No. 5026

For price and order information, please call one of our Telephone Representatives. Ask for a free catalog describing more than 1,000 items available through Hazelden Educational Materials.

HAZELDEN EDUCATIONAL MATERIALS

1-800-328-9000 **1-800-257-0070** **1-612-257-4010**
(Toll Free. U.S. Only) (Toll Free. MN Only) (AK and Outside U.S.)

Pleasant Valley Road • **P.O. Box 176** • **Center City, MN 55012-0176**